Henry Thayer Niles

The Dawn and the Day

Or, the Buddha and the Christ. Part I

Henry Thayer Niles

The Dawn and the Day
Or, the Buddha and the Christ. Part I

ISBN/EAN: 9783337246419

Printed in Europe, USA, Canada, Australia, Japan

Cover: Foto ©Lupo / pixelio.de

More available books at **www.hansebooks.com**

THE DAWN AND THE DAY

OR

THE BUDDHA AND THE CHRIST

PART I

BY

HENRY T. NILES

1894

Copyright, 1894,
By HENRY T. NILES.
All rights reserved.

THE BLADE PRINTING & PAPER COMPANY,
TOLEDO, OHIO

PREFACE.

When Humboldt first ascended the Andes and saw the trees, shrubs and flora he had long before studied on the Alps, he had only to look at his barometer, or at the sea of mountains and hills below, the rocks and soil around, and the sun above, to understand this seeming marvel of creation; while those who knew less of the laws of order and universal harmony might be lost in conjectures about pollen floating in the upper air, or seeds carried by birds across seas, forgetting that preservation is perpetual creation, and that it takes no more power to clothe a mountain just risen from the sea in appropriate verdure than to renew the beauty and the bloom of spring.

Max Mueller, who looks through antiquity with the same clear vision with which Humboldt examined the physical world, when he found the most ancient Hindoos bowing in worship before Dyaus Pitar, the exact equivalent of the Zeus Pater of the Greeks and the Jupiter of the Romans, and of "Our Father who art in the heavens" in our own divinely taught prayer, instead of indulging in wild speculations about the chance belief of some ancient chief or patriarch, transmitted across continents and seas and even across the great gulf that has always divided the Aryan from the Semitic civilization and preserved through ages of darkness and unbelief, saw in it the common yearning of the human soul to find rest on a loving Father's almighty arm; yet when our oriental missionaries and scholars found such fundamental truths of their own religion as the common brotherhood of man, and that love is the vital force of all religion, which consists not in blood-oblations or in forms and creeds, but in shunning evil and doing good, and that we must overcome evil by good and hatred by love, and that there is a spiritual world and life after death embodied in the teachings of Buddha — instead of finding in this great fact new proof of the common Father's love for all His children, they immediately began to indulge in conjectures as to how these truths might have been derived from the early Christians who visited the East, while those who were disposed to reject the claims of Christianity have exhausted research and conjecture to find something looking as if Christianity itself might have been derived from the Buddhist missionaries to Palestine and Egypt, both overlooking the remarkable fact that it is only in fundamental truths that the two religions agree, while in the dogmas, legends, creeds and speculations which form the wall of separation between them they are as wide asunder as the poles.

How comes it on the one theory that the Nestorians, whose peculiar creed had already separated them from the balance of the Christian church, taught their Buddhist disciples no part of that creed to which they have adhered with such tenacity through the ages? And on the other theory, how comes it, if the Divine Master was, as some modern writers claim, an Essene, that is, a Buddhist monk, that there is not in all his teachings a trace of the speculations and legends which had already buried the fundamental truths of Buddhism almost out of sight?

How sad to hear a distinguished Christian scholar like Sir Monier Williams cautioning his readers against giving a Christian meaning to the Christian expressions he constantly met with in Buddhism, and yet informing them that a learned and distinguished Japanese gentleman told him it was a source of great delight to him to find so many of his most cherished religious beliefs in the New Testament; and to see an earnest Christian missionary like good Father Huc, when in the busy city of Lha-ssa, on the approach of evening, at the sound of a bell the whole population sunk on their knees in a concert of prayer, only finding in it an attempt of Satan to counterfeit Christian worship; and on the other hand to see ancient and modern learning ransacked to prove that the brightest and clearest light that ever burst upon a sinful and benighted world was but the reflected rays of another faith.

And yet this same Sir Monier Williams says: "We shall not be far wrong in attempting an outline of the Buddha's life if we begin by assuming that intense individuality, fervid earnestness and severe simplicity, combined with singular beauty of countenance, calm dignity of bearing, and almost superhuman persuasiveness of speech, were conspicuous in the great teacher." To believe that such a character was the product of a false religion, or that he was given over to believe a lie, savors too much of that worst agnosticism which would in effect deny the universality of God's love and would limit His care to some favored locality or age or race.

How much more in harmony with the broad philosophy of such men as Humboldt and Mueller, and with the character of a loving Father, to believe that at all times and in all countries He has been watching over all His children and giving them all the light they were capable of receiving.

This narrow view is especially out of place in treating of Buddhism and Christianity, as Buddha himself predicted that his Dharma would last but five hundred years, when he would be succeeded by Matreya, that is, Love incarnate, on which account the whole Buddhist world was on tiptoe of expectation at the time of the coming of our Lord, so that the wise men of the East were not only following their guiding-star but the prediction of their own great prophet in seeking Bethlehem.

Had the Christian missionaries to the East left behind them their creeds, which have only served to divide Christians into hostile sects and sometimes into hostile camps, and which so far as I can see, after years of patient study, have no necessary connection with the simple, living truths taught by our Saviour, and had taken only their New Testaments and their earnest desire to do good, the history of missions would have been widely different.

How of the earth earthy seemed the walls that divided the delegates to the world's great Congress of Religions, recently held in Chicago, and how altogether divine

> The love which like an endless golden chain
> Joined all in one.

Whatever others may think, it is my firm belief that Buddhism and Christianity, which we cannot doubt have influenced for good such vast masses the human family, both descended from heaven clothed in robes of celestial purity which have become sadly stained by their contact with the selfishness of a sinful world, except for which belief the following pages would never have been written, which are now sent forth in the hope that they may do something to enable Buddhists and Christians to see eye to eye and something to promote peace and good-will among men.

While following my own conceptions and even fancies in many things, I believe the leading characters and incidents to be historical, and I have given nothing as the teaching of the great master which was not to my mind clearly authenticated.

To those who have read so much about agnostic Buddhism, and about Nirvana meaning annihilation, it may seem bold in me to present Buddha as an undoubting believer in the fundamental truths of all religion, and as not only a believer in a spiritual world but an actual visitor to its sad and blissful scenes; but the only agnosticism I have been able to trace to Buddha was a want of faith in the many ways invented through the ages to escape the consequences of sin and to avoid the necessity of personal purification, and the only annihilation he taught and yearned for was the annihilation of self in the highest Christian sense, and escape from that body of death from which the Apostle Paul so earnestly sought deliverance.

Doubtless agnosticism and almost every form of belief and unbelief subsequently sprang up among the intensely acute and speculative peoples of the East known under the general name of Buddhists, as they did among the less acute and speculative peoples of the West known as Christians; but the one is no more primitive Buddhism than the other is primitive Christianity.

While there are innumerable poetic legends—of which Spence Hardy's "Manual of Buddhism" is a great storehouse, and many of which are given by Arnold in his beautiful poem—strewn thick along the track of Buddhist literature, constantly tempting one to leave the straight path of the development of a great religion, I have carefully avoided what did not commend itself to my mind as either historical or spiritual truth.

It was my original design to follow the wonderful career of Buddha until his long life closed with visions of the golden city much as described in Revelation, and then to follow that most wonderful career of Buddhist missions, not only through India and Ceylon, but to Palestine, Greece and Egypt, and over the table-lands of Asia and through the Chinese Empire to Japan, and thence by the black stream to Mexico and Central America, and then to follow the wise men of the East until the Light of the world dawned on them on the plains of Bethlehem—a task but half accomplished, which I shall yet complete if life and strength are spared.

A valued literary friend suggests that the social life described in the following pages is too much like ours, but why should their daily life and social customs be greatly different from ours? The Aryan migrations to India and to Europe were in large masses, of course taking their social customs, or as the Romans would say, their household gods, with them.

What wonder, then, that the home as Tacitus describes it in the "Wilds of Germany" was substantially what Mueller finds from the very structure of the Sanscrit and European languages it must have been in Bactria, the common cradle of the Aryan race. There can scarcely be a doubt that twenty-five hundred years ago the daily life and social customs in the north of India, which had been under undisputed Aryan control long enough for the Sanscrit language to spring up, come to perfection and finally become obsolete, were more like ours than like those of modern India after the many — and especially the Mohammedan — conquests and after centuries of oppression and alien rule.

If a thousand English-speaking Aryans should now be placed on some distant island, how much would their social customs and even amusements differ from ours in a hundred years? Only so far as changed climate and surroundings compelled.

I give as an introduction an outline of the golden, silver, brazen and iron ages, as described by the ancient poets and believed in by all antiquity, as it was in the very depths of the darkness of the iron age that our great light appeared in Northern India. The very denseness of the darkness of the age in which he came makes the clearness of the light more wonderful, and accounts for the joy with which it was received and the rapidity with which it spread.

Not to enter into the niceties of chronological questions, the mission of Buddha may be roughly said to have commenced about five hundred years before the commencement of our era, and with incessant labors and long and repeated journeys to have lasted forty-five years, when at about the age of eighty he died, or, as the Buddhists more truthfully and more beautifully say, entered Nirvana.

HENRY T. NILES.

TOLEDO, January 1, 1894.

Since this work was in the hands of the printer I have read the recent work of Bishop Copelston, of Columbo, Ceylon, and it was a source of no small gratification to find him in all material points agreeing with the result of my somewhat extensive investigations as given within, for in Ceylon, if anywhere, we would expect accuracy. Here the great Buddhist development first comes in contact with authentic history during the third century B. C. in the reign of the great Asoka, the discovery of whose rock inscriptions shed such a flood of light on primitive Buddhism, while it still retained enough of its primitive power, as we learn from those inscriptions themselves, to turn that monarch from a course of cruel tyranny, and, as we learn from the history of Ceylon, to induce his son and daughter to abandon royalty and become the first missionaries to that beautiful island.

H. T. N.

INTRODUCTION.

The golden age — when men were brothers all,
The golden rule their law and God their king;
When no fierce beasts did through the forests roam,
Nor poisonous reptiles crawl upon the ground;
When trees bore only wholesome, luscious fruits,
And thornless roses breathed their sweet perfumes;
When sickness, sin and sorrow were unknown,
And tears but spoke of joy too deep for words;
When painless death but led to higher life,
A life that knows no end, in that bright world
Whence angels on the ladder Jacob saw,
Descending, talk with man as friend to friend —
That age of purity and peace had passed,
But left a living memory behind,
Cherished and handed down from sire to son
Through all the scattered peoples of the earth,
A living prophecy of what this world,
This sad and sinful world, might yet become.

The silver age — an age of faith, not sight —
Came next, when reason ruled instead of love;
When men as through a glass but darkly saw
What to their fathers clearly stood revealed
In God's own light of love-illumined truth,
Of which the sun that rising paints the east,
And whose last rays with glory gild the west,
Is but an outbirth. Then were temples reared,
And priests 'mid clouds of incense sang His praise
Who out of densest darkness called the light,
And from His own unbounded fullness made
The heavens and earth and all that in them is.
Then landmarks were first set, lest men contend
For God's free gifts, that all in peace had shared.
Then laws were made to govern those whose sires
Were laws unto themselves. Then sickness came,
And grief and pain attended men from birth to
　　death.
But still a silver light lined every cloud,
And hope was given to cheer and comfort men.

　　The brazen age, brilliant but cold, succeeds.
This was an age of knowledge, art and war,
When the knights-errant of the ancient world,
Adventures seeking, roamed with brazen swords
Which by a wondrous art — then known, now lost —
Were hard as flint, and edged to cut a hair

Or cleave in twain a warrior armor-clad
And armed with shields adorned by Vulcan's art,
Wonder of coming times and theme for bards.*
Then science searched through nature's heights
    and depths.
Heaven's canopy thick set with stars was mapped,
The constellations named, and all the laws searched
    out
That guide their motions, rolling sphere on sphere.†
Then men by reasonings piled up mountain high
Thought to scale heaven, and to dethrone heaven's
    king,
Whose imitators weak, with quips and quirks
And ridicule would now destroy all sacred things.
This age great Homer and old Hesiod sang,
And gods they made of hero, artist, bard.

  At length this twilight of the ages fades,
And starless night now sinks upon the world —
An age of iron, cruel, dark and cold.
On Asia first this outer darkness fell,
Once seat of paradise, primordial peace,
Perennial harmony and perfect love.
A despot's will was then a nation's law;

---

    * See Hesiod's description of the shield of Hercules, the St George of that ancient age of chivalry.

    † See the celebrated zodiac of Denderah, given in Landseer's "Sabæan Researches," and in Napoleon's "Egypt."

An idol's car crushed out poor human lives,
And human blood polluted many shrines.
Then human speculation made of God
A shoreless ocean, distant, waveless, vast,
Of truth that sees not and unfeeling love,
Whence souls as drops were taken back to fall,
Absorbed and lost, when, countless ages passed,
They should complete their round as souls of men,
Of beasts, of birds and of all creeping things.
And, even worse, the cruel iron castes,
One caste too holy for another's touch,
Had every human aspiration crushed,
The common brotherhood of man destroyed,
And made all men but Pharisees or slaves.
And worst of all — and what could e'en be worse? —
Woman, bone of man's bone, flesh of his flesh,
The equal partner of a double life,
Who in the world's best days stood by his side
To lighten every care, and heighten every joy,
And in the world's decline still clung to him,
She only true when all beside were false,
When all were cruel she alone still kind,
Light of his hearth and mistress of his home,
Sole spot where peace and joy could still be found —
Woman herself cast down, despised was made
Slave to man's luxury and brutal lust.

Then war was rapine, havoc, needless blood,
Infants impaled before their mothers' eyes,
Women dishonored, mutilated, slain,
Parents but spared to see their children die.
Then peace was but a faithless, hollow truce,
With plots and counter-plots; the dagger's point
And poisoned cup instead of open war;
And life a savage, grim conspiracy
Of mutual murder, treachery and greed.
O dark and cruel age! O cruel creeds!
O cruel men! O crushed and bleeding hearts,
That from the very ground in anguish cry:
"Is there no light — no hope — no help — no God?"

The Dawn and the Day

---OR---

THE BUDDHA AND THE CHRIST.

BOOK I.

Northward from Ganges' stream and India's plains
An ancient city crowned a lofty hill,
Whose high embattled walls had often rolled
The surging, angry tide of battle back.
Walled on three sides, but on the north a cliff,
At once the city's quarry and its guard,
Cut out in galleries, with vaulted roofs*
Upborne upon cyclopean columns vast,
Chiseled with art, their capitals adorned
With lions, elephants, and bulls, life size,
Once dedicate to many monstrous gods

---

*Lieutenant-General Briggs, in his lectures on the aboriginal races of India, says the Hindoos themselves refer the excavation of caves and temples to the period of the aboriginal kings.

Before the Aryan race as victors came,
Then prisons, granaries and magazines,
Now only known to bandits and wild beasts.
This cliff, extending at each end, bends north,
And rises in two mountain-chains that end
In two vast snow-capped Himalayan peaks,
Between which runs a glittering glacial stream,
A mighty moving mass of crystal ice,
Crushing the rocks in its resistless course;
From which bursts forth a river that had made
Of all this valley one great highland lake,
Which on one side had burst its bounds and cut
In myriad years a channel through the rock,
So narrow that a goat might almost leap
From cliff to cliff—these cliffs so smooth and steep
The eagles scarce could build upon their sides;
This yawning chasm so deep one scarce could hear
The angry waters roaring far below.

    This stream, guided by art, now fed a lake
Above the city and behind this cliff,
Which, guided thence in channels through the rock,
Fed many fountains, sending crystal streams
Through every street and down the terraced hill,
And through the plain in little silver streams,
Spreading the richest verdure far and wide.*
Here was the seat of King Suddhodana,
His royal park, walled by eternal hills,

---

*The art of irrigation, once practiced on such a mighty scale, now seems practically a lost art but just now being revived on our western plains.

Where trees and shrubs and flowers all native grew ;
For in its bounds all the four seasons met,
From ever-laughing, ever-blooming spring
To savage winter with eternal snows.
Here stately palms, the banyan's many trunks,
Darkening whole acres with its grateful shade,
And bamboo groves, with graceful waving plumes,
The champak, with its fragrant golden flowers,
Asokas, one bright blaze of brilliant bloom,
The mohra, yielding food and oil and wine,
The sacred sandal and the spreading oak,
The mountain-loving fir and spruce and pine,
And giant cedars, grandest of them all,
Planted in ages past, and thinned and pruned
With that high art that hides all trace of art,*
Were placed to please the eye and show their form
In groves, in clumps, in jungles and alone.

Here all a forest seemed ; there open groves,
With vine-clad trees, vines hanging from each limb,
A pendant chain of bloom, with shaded drives
And walks, with rustic seats, cool grots and dells,
With fountains playing and with babbling brooks,
And stately swans sailing on little lakes,
While peacocks, rainbow-tinted shrikes, pheasants,
Glittering like precious stones, parrots, and birds
Of all rich plumage, fly from tree to tree,
The whole scene vocal with sweet varied song ;

* " And, that which all faire workes doth most aggrace,
   The art, which all that wrought, appeared in no place."
                         —Faerie Queene, B. 2, Canto 12.

And here a widespread lawn bedecked with flowers,
With clumps of brilliant roses grown to trees,
And fields with dahlias spread,* not stiff and prim
Like the starched ruffle of an ancient dame,
But growing in luxuriance rich and wild,
The colors of the evening and the rainbow joined,
White, scarlet, yellow, crimson, deep maroon,
Blending all colors in one dazzling blaze:
There orchards bend beneath their luscious loads;
Here vineyards climb the hills thick set with grapes;
There rolling pastures spread, where royal mares,
High bred, and colts too young for bit or spur,
Now quiet feed, then, as at trumpet's call,
With lion bounds, tails floating, necks outstretched,†
Nostrils distended, fleet as the flying wind
They skim the plain, and sweep in circles wide—
Nature's Olympic, copied, ne'er excelled.
Here, deer with dappled fawn bound o'er the grass,‡
And sacred herds, and sheep with skipping lambs;
There, great white elephants in quiet nooks;
While high on cliffs framed in with living green
Goats climb and seem to hang and feed in air—
Sweet spot, with all to please and nothing to offend.

---

* See Miss Gordon Cumming's descriptions of the fields of wild dahlias in Northern India.

† By far the finest display of the mettle and blood of high-bred horses I have ever seen has been in the pasture field, and this description is drawn from life

‡ Once, coming upon a little prairie in the midst of a great forest, I saw a herd of startled deer bound over the grass, a scene never to be forgotten.

Here on a hill the royal palace stood,
A gem of art; and near, another hill,
Its top crowned by an aged banyan tree,
Its sides clad in strange jyotismati grass,*
By day a sober brown, but in the night
Glowing as if the hill were all aflame —
Twin wonders to the dwellers in the plain,
Their guides and landmarks day and night,
This glittering palace and this glowing hill.
Within, above the palace rose a tower,
Which memory knew but as the ancient tower,
Foursquare and high, an altar and a shrine
On its broad top, where burned perpetual fire,
Emblem of boundless and eternal love
And truth that knows no night, no cloud, no change,
Long since gone out, with that most ancient faith
In one great Father, source of life and light.†
Still round this ancient tower, strange hopes and
    fears,
And memories handed down from sire to son,
Were clustered thick. An army, old men say,
Once camped against the city, when strange lights
Burst from this tower, blinding their dazzled eyes.
They fled amazed, nor dared to look behind.
The people bloody war and cruel bondage saw
On every side, and they at peace and free,
And thought a power to save dwelt in that tower.

---

*See Miss Gordon Cumming's description of a hill covered with this luminous grass.

†There can be no doubt that the fire-worship of the East is the remains of a true but largely emblematic religion.

And now strange prophecies and sayings old
Were everywhere rehearsed, that from this hill
Should come a king or savior of the world.
Even the poor dwellers in the distant plain
Looked up; they too had heard that hence should come
One quick to hear the poor and strong to save.
And who shall dare to chide their simple faith?
This humble reverence for the great unknown
Brings men near God, and opens unseen worlds,
Whence comes all life, and where all power doth dwell.

   Morning and evening on this tower the king,
Before the rising and the setting sun,
Blindly, but in his father's faith, bowed down.
Then he would rise and on his kingdom gaze.
East, west, hills beyond hills stretched far away,
Wooded, terraced, or bleak and bald and bare,
Till in dim distance all were leveled lost.
One rich and varied carpet spread far south,
Of fields, of groves, of busy cities wrought,
With mighty rivers seeming silver threads;
And to the north the Himalayan chain,
Peak beyond peak, a wall of crest and crag,
Ice bound, snow capped, backed by intensest blue,
Untrod, immense, that, like a crystal wall,
In myriad varied tints the glorious light
Of rising and of setting sun reflects;
His noble city lying at his feet,

And his broad park, tinged by the sun's slant rays
A thousand softly rich and varied shades.

    Still on this scene of grandeur, plenty, peace
And ever-varying beauty, he would gaze
With sadness. He had heard these prophecies,
And felt the unrest in that great world within,
Hid from our blinded eyes, yet ever near,
The very soul and life of this dead world,
Which seers and prophets open-eyed have seen,
On which the dying often raptured gaze,
And where they live when they are mourned as dead.
This world was now astir, foretelling day.
"A king shall come, they say, to rule the world,
If he will rule ; but whence this mighty king?
My years decline apace, and yet no son
Of mine to rule or light my funeral pile."

    One night Queen Maya, sleeping by her lord,
Dreamed a strange dream; she dreamed she saw a star
Gliding from heaven and resting over her;
She dreamed she heard strange music, soft and sweet,
So distant "joy and peace" was all she heard.
In joy and peace she wakes, and waits to know
What this strange dream might mean, and whence
    it came.

    Drums, shells and trumpets sound for joy, not
    war;
The streets are swept and sprinkled with perfumes,
And myriad lamps shine from each house and tree,

And myriad flags flutter in every breeze,
And children crowned with flowers dance in the
 streets,
And all keep universal holiday
With shows and games, and laugh and dance and
 song,
For to the gentle queen a son is born,
To King Suddhodana the good an heir.

But scarcely had these myriad lamps gone out,
The sounds of revelry had scarcely died,
When coming from the palace in hot haste,
One cried, "Maya, the gentle queen, is dead."
Then mirth was changed to sadness, joy to grief,
For all had learned to love the gentle queen —
But at Siddartha's birth this was foretold.

Among the strangers bringing gifts from far,
There came an ancient sage — whence, no one knew —
Age-bowed, head like the snow, eyes filmed and
 white,
So deaf the thunder scarcely startled him,
Who met them, as they said, three journeys back,
And all his talk was of a new-born king,
Just born, to rule the world if he would rule.
He was so gentle, seemed so wondrous wise,
They followed him, he following, he said,
A light they could not see; and when encamped,
Morn, noon and night devoutly would he pray,
And then would talk for hours, as friend to friend,
With questionings about this new-born king,

Gazing intently at the tent's blank wall,
With nods and smiles, as if he saw and heard,
While they sit lost in wonder, as one sits
Who never saw a telephone, but hears
Unanswered questions, laughter at unheard jests,
And sees one bid a little box good-by.
And when they came before the king, they saw,
Laughing and cooing on its mother's knee,
Picture of innocence, a sweet young child;
He saw a mighty prophet, and bowed down
Eight times in reverence to the very ground,
And rising said, "Thrice happy house, all hail!
This child would rule the world, if he would rule,
But he, too good to rule, is born to save;
But Maya's work is done, the dēvas wait."
But when they sought for him, the sage was gone,
Whence come or whither gone none ever knew.
Then gentle Maya understood her dream.
The music nearer, clearer sounds; she sleeps.
But when the funeral pile was raised for her,
Of aloe, sandal, and all fragrant woods,
And decked with flowers and rich with rare perfumes,
And when the queen was gently laid thereon,
As in sweet sleep, and the pile set aflame,
The king cried out in anguish; when the sage
Again appeared, and gently said, "Weep not!
Seek not, O king, the living with the dead!
'Tis but her cast-off garment, not herself,
That now dissolves in air. Thy loved one lives,

Become thy deva,* who was erst thy queen."
This said, he vanished, and was no more seen.

Now other hands take up that mother's task.
Another breast nurses that sweet young child
With growing love; for who can nurse a child,
Feel its warm breath, and little dimpled hands,
Kiss its soft lips, look in its laughing eyes,
Hear its low-cooing love-notes soft and sweet,
And not feel something of that miracle,
A mother's love—so old yet ever new,
Stronger than death, bravest among the brave,
Gentle as brave, watchful both night and day,
That never changes, never tires nor sleeps.
Whence comes this wondrous and undying love?
Whence can it come, unless it comes from heaven,
Whose life is love — eternal, perfect love!

From babe to boy, from boy to youth he grew,
But more in grace and knowledge than in years.
At play his joyous laugh rang loud and clear,
His foot was fleetest in all boyish games,
And strong his arm, and steady nerve and eye,
To whirl the quoit and send the arrow home;
Yet seeming oft to strive, he'd check his speed
And miss his mark to let a comrade win.
In fullness of young life he climbed the cliffs
Where human foot had never trod before.
He led the chase, but when soft-eyed gazelles

* The difference between the Buddhist idea of a deva and the Christian idea of an attendant angel is scarcely perceptible.

Or bounding deer, or any harmless thing,
Came in the range of his unerring dart,
He let them pass; for why, thought he, should men
In wantonness make war on innocence?

   One day the Prince Siddartha saw the grooms
Gathered about a stallion, snowy white,
Descended from that great Nisæan stock
His fathers brought from Iran's distant plain,
Named Kantaka. Some held him fast with chains
Till one could mount. He, like a lion snared,
Frantic with rage and fear, did fiercely bound.
They cut his tender mouth with bloody bit,
Beating his foaming sides until the Prince,
Sterner than was his wont, bade them desist,
While he spoke soothingly, patted his head
And stroked his neck, and dropped those galling
    chains,
When Kantaka's fierce flaming eyes grew mild,
He quiet stood, by gentleness subdued—
Such mighty power hath gentleness and love—
And from that day no horse so strong and fleet,
So kind and true, easy to check and guide,
As Kantaka, Siddartha's noble steed.

   To playmates he was gentle as a girl;
Yet should the strong presume upon their strength
To overbear or wrong those weaker than them-
    selves,
His sturdy arm and steady eye checked them,
And he would gently say, "Brother, not so;

Our strength was given to aid and not oppress."
For in an ancient book he found a truth —
A book no longer read, a truth forgot,
Entombed in iron castes, and buried deep
In speculations and in subtle creeds —
That men, high, low, rich, poor, are brothers all,*
Which, pondered much in his heart's fruitful soil,
Had taken root as a great living truth
That to a mighty doctrine soon would grow,
A mighty tree to heal the nations with its leaves —
Like some small grain of wheat, appearing dead,
In mummy-case three thousand years ago†
Securely wrapped and sunk in Egypt's tombs,
Themselves buried beneath the desert sands,
Which now brought forth, and planted in fresh soil,
And watered by the dews and rains of heaven,
Shoots up and yields a hundred-fold of grain,
Until in golden harvests now it waves
On myriad acres, many thousand miles
From where the single ancient seed had grown.

Thus he grew up with all that heart could wish
Or power command; his very life itself,
So fresh and young, sound body with sound mind,
The living fountain of perpetual joy.
Yet he would often sit and sadly think
Sad thoughts and deep, and far beyond his years;

---

*The Brahmans claim that Buddha's great doctrine of universal brotherhood was taken from their sacred books and was not an originality of Buddha, as his followers claim.

†The Mediteranean or Egyptian wheat is said to have this origin.

How sorrow filled the world; how things were
    shared —
One born to waste, another born to want;
One for life's cream, others to drain its dregs;
One born a master, others abject slaves.
And when he asked his masters to explain,
When all were brothers, how such things could be,
They gave him speculations, fables old,
How Brahm first Brahmans made to think for all,
And then Kshatriyas, warriors from their birth,
Then Sudras, to draw water and hew wood.
"But why should one for others think, when all
Must answer for themselves? Why brothers fight?
And why one born another's slave, when all
Might serve and help each other?" he would ask.
But they could only answer: "Never doubt,
For so the holy Brahmans always taught."
Still he must think, and as he thought he sighed,
Not for his petty griefs that last an hour,
But for the bitter sorrows of the world
That crush all men, and last from age to age.

    The good old king saw this—saw that the prince,
The apple of his eye, dearer than life,
Stately in form, supple and strong in limb,
Quick to learn every art of peace and war,
Displaying and excelling every grace
And attribute of his most royal line,
Whom all would follow whereso'er he led,
So fit to rule the world if he would rule,
Thought less of ruling than of saving men.

He saw the glory of his ancient house
Suspended on an if — if he will rule
The empire of the world, and power to crush
Those cruel, bloody kings who curse mankind,
And power to make a universal peace;
If not this high career, with glory crowned,
Then seeking truth through folly's devious ways;
By self-inflicted torture seeking bliss,
And by self-murder seeking higher life;
On one foot standing till the other pine,
Arms stretched aloft, fingers grown bloodless claws,
Or else, impaled on spikes, with festering sores
Covered from head to foot, the body wastes
With constant anguish and with slow decay.*
"Can this be wisdom? Can such a life be good
That shuns all duties lying in our path —
Useless to others, filled with grief and pain?
Not so my father's god teaches to live.
Rising each morning most exact in time,
He bathes the earth and sky with rosy light
And fills all nature with new life and joy;
The cock's shrill clarion calls us to awake
And breathe this life and hear the bursts of song
That fill each grove, inhale the rich perfume
Of opening flowers, and work while day shall last.
Then rising higher, he warms each dank, cold spot,

---

* At the time of Buddha's birth there seemed to be no mean between the Chakravartin or absolute monarch and the recluse who had renounced all ordinary duties and enjoyments, and was subjecting himself to all deprivations and sufferings. Buddha taught the middle course of diligence in daily duties and universal love.

Dispels the sickening vapors, clothes the fields
With waving grain, the trees with golden fruit,
The vines with grapes; and when 'tis time for rest,
Sinks in the west, and with new glory gilds
The mountain-tops, the clouds and western sky,
And calls all nature to refreshing sleep.
If he be God, the useful are like God;
If not, God made the sun, who made all men
And by his great example teaches them
The diligent are wise, the useful good."

Sorely perplexed he called his counselors,
Grown gray in serving their beloved king,
And said: "Friends of my youth, manhood and age,
So wise in counsel and so brave in war,
Who never failed in danger or distress,
Oppressed with fear, I come to you for aid.
You know the prophecies, that from my house
Shall come a king, or savior of the world.
You saw strange signs precede Siddartha's birth,
And saw the ancient sage whom no one knew
Fall down before the prince, and hail my house.
You heard him tell the queen she soon would die,
And saw her sink in death as in sweet sleep;
You laid her gently on her funeral pile,
And heard my cry of anguish, when the sage
Again appeared and bade me not to weep
For her as dead who lived and loved me still.
We saw the prince grow up to man's estate,
So strong and full of manliness and grace,

And wise beyond his teachers and his years,
And thought in him the prophecies fulfilled,
And that with glory he would rule the world
And bless all men with universal peace.
But now dark shadows fall athwart our hopes.
Often in sleep the prince will start and cry
As if in pain, 'O world, sad world, I come!'
But roused, he'll sometimes sit the livelong day,
Forgetting teachers, sports and even food,
As if with dreadful visions overwhelmed,
Or buried in great thoughts profound and deep.
But yet to see our people, riding forth,
To their acclaims he answers with such grace
And gentle stateliness, my heart would swell
As I would hear the people to each other say:
'Who ever saw such grace and grandeur joined?'
Yet while he answers gladness with like joy,
His eyes seem searching for the sick and old,
The poor, and maimed, and blind — all forms of grief.
And oft he'd say, tears streaming from his eyes,*
'Let us return; my heart can bear no more.'

---

* I am aware that some Buddhist authors whom Arnold has followed in his "Light of Asia" make Buddha but little better than a state prisoner, and would have us believe that the glimpses he got of the ills that flesh is heir to were gained in spite of all precautions, as he was occasionally taken out of his rose embowered, damsel filled prison-house, and not as any prince of high intelligence and tender sensibilities who loved his people and mingled freely with them would gain a knowledge of suffering and sorrow; but we are justified in passing all such fancies, not only on account of their intrinsic improbability, but because the great Asvaghosha, who wrote about the beginning of our era, knew nothing of them.

One day we saw beneath a peepul-tree
An aged Brahman, wasted with long fasts,
Loathsome with self-inflicted ghastly wounds,
A rigid skeleton, standing erect,
One hand stretched out, the other stretched aloft,
His long white beard grown filthy by neglect.
Whereat the prince with shuddering horror shook,
And cried, 'O world! must I be such for thee?'
And once he led the chase of a wild boar
In the great forest near the glacier's foot;
On Kantaka so fleet he soon outstripped
The rest, and in the distance disappeared.
But when at night they reached the rendezvous,
Siddartha was not there; and through the night
They searched, fearing to find their much loved
  prince
A mangled corpse under some towering cliff,
But searched in vain, and searched again next day,
Till in despair they thought to bring me word
The prince was lost, when Kantaka was seen
Loose-reined and free, and near Siddartha sat
Under a giant cedar's spreading shade.
Absorbed in thought, in contemplation lost,
Unconscious that a day and night had passed.
I cannot reason with such earnestness —
I dare not chide such deep and tender love,
But much I fear his reason's overthrow
Or that he may become like that recluse
He shuddered at, and not a mighty king
With power to crush the wrong and aid the right.
How can we turn his mind from such sad thoughts

To life's full joys, the duties of a king,
And his great destiny so long foretold?"

  The oldest and the wisest answered him:
"Most noble king, your thoughts have long been
    mine.
Oft have I seen him lost in musings sad,
And overwhelmed with this absorbing love.
I know no cure for such corroding thoughts
But thoughts less sad, for such absorbing love
But stronger love."
              "But how awake such thoughts?"
The king replied. "How kindle such a love?
His loves seem but as phosphorescent flames
That skim the surface, leaving him heart-whole—
All but this deep and all-embracing love
That folds within its arms a suffering world."

  "Yes, noble king, so roams the antlered deer,
Adding each year a branch to his great horns,
Until the unseen archer lays him low.
So lives our prince; but he may see the day
Two laughing eyes shall pierce his inmost soul,
And make his whole frame quiver with new fire.
The next full moon he reaches man's estate.
We all remember fifty years ago
When you became a man, the sports and games,
The contests of fair women and brave men,
In beauty, arts and arms, that filled three days
With joy and gladness, music, dance and song.
Let us with double splendor now repeat

That festival, with prizes that shall draw
From all your kingdom and the neighbor states
Their fairest women and their bravest men.
If any chance shall bring his destined mate,
You then shall see love dart from eye to eye,
As darts the lightning's flash from cloud to cloud."
And this seemed good, and so was ordered done.

The king to all his kingdom couriers sent,
And to the neighbor states, inviting all
To a great festival and royal games
The next full moon, day of Siddartha's birth,
And offering varied prizes, rich and rare,
To all in feats of strength and speed and skill,
And prizes doubly rich and doubly rare
To all such maidens fair as should compete
In youth and beauty, whencesoe'er they came,
The prince to be the judge and give the prize.

Now all was joy and bustle in the streets,
And joy and stir in palace and in park,
The prince himself joining the joyful throng,
Forgetting now the sorrows of the world.
Devising and directing new delights
Until the park became a fairy scene.

Behind the palace lay a maidan wide
For exercise in arms and manly sports,
Its sides bordered by gently rising hills,
Where at their ease the city's myriads sat
Under the shade of high-pruned spreading trees,

Fanned by cool breezes from the snow-capped peaks;
While north, and next the lake, a stately dome
Stood out, on slender, graceful columns raised,
With seats, rank above rank, in order placed,
The throne above, and near the throne were bowers
Of slender lattice-work, with trailing vines,
Thick set with flowers of every varied tint,
Breathing perfumes, where beauty's champions
Might sit, unseen of all yet seeing all.

At length Siddartha's natal day arrives
With joy to rich and poor, to old and young —
Not joy that wealth can buy or power command,
But real joy, that springs from real love,
Love to the good old king and noble prince.

When dawning day tinges with rosy light
The snow-capped peaks of Himalaya's chain,
The people are astir. In social groups,
The old and young, companions, neighbors, friends,
Baskets well filled, they choose each vantage-
　　ground,
Until each hill a sea of faces shows,
A sea of sparkling joy and rippling mirth.

At trumpet-sound all eyes are eager turned
Up toward the palace gates, now open wide,
From whence a gay procession issues forth,
A chorus of musicians coming first,
And next the prince mounted on Kantaka;
Then all the high-born youth in rich attire,

Mounted on prancing steeds with trappings gay;
And then the good old king, in royal state,
On his huge elephant, white as the snow,
Surrounded by his aged counselors,
Some on their chargers, some in litters borne,
Their long white beards floating in every breeze;
And next, competitors for every prize:
Twelve archers, who could pierce the lofty swans
Sailing from feeding-grounds by distant seas
To summer nests by Thibet's marshy lakes,
Or hit the whirring pheasant as it flies —
For in this peaceful reign they did not make
Men targets for their art, and armor-joints
The marks through which to pierce and kill;
Then wrestlers, boxers, those who hurl the quoit,
And runners fleet, both lithe and light of limb;
And then twelve mighty spearmen, who could pierce
The fleeing boar or deer or fleet gazelle;
Then chariots, three horses yoked to each,
The charioteers in Persian tunics clad,
Arms bare, legs bare — all were athletes in power,
In form and grace each an Apollo seemed;
Yoked to the first were three Nisæan steeds,*

---

* To suppose that the Aryan races when they emigrated to India or Europe left behind them their most valuable possession, the Nisæan horse, is to suppose them lacking in the qualities of thrift and shrewdness which have distinguished their descendants. That the Nisæan horse of the table-lands of Asia was the horse of the armored knights of the middle ages and substantially the Percheron horse of France, I had a curious proof: In Layard's Nineveh is a picture of a Nisæan horse found among the ruins, which would have been taken as a good picture of a Percheron stallion I once owned, who stood for the picture here drawn of what I regard as his undoubted ancestor.

Each snowy white, proud stepping, rangy, tall,
Chests broad, legs clean and strong, necks arched
 and high,
With foreheads broad, and eyes large, full and mild,
A race that oft Olympic prizes won,
And whose descendants far from Iran's plains
Bore armored knights in battle's deadly shock
On many bloody European fields;
Then three of ancient Babylonian stock,*
Blood bay and glossy as rich Tyrian silk —
Such horses Israel's sacred prophets saw
Bearing their conquerors in triumph home,
A race for ages kept distinct and pure,
Fabled from Alexander's charger sprung;
Then three from distant desert Tartar steppes,
Ewe-necked, ill-favored creatures, lank and gaunt,
That made the people laugh as they passed by —
Who ceased to laugh when they had run the race —
Such horses bore the mighty Mongol hosts†
That with the cyclone's speed swept o'er the earth;
Then three, one gray, one bay, one glossy black,
Descended from four horses long since brought
By love-sick chief from Araby the blest,
Seeking with such rare gifts an Indian bride.
Whose slender, graceful forms, compact and light,
Combined endurance, beauty, strength and speed —

---

* Marco Polo speaks of the breed of horses here attempted to be described as "excellent, large, strong and swift, said to be of the race of Alexander's Bucephalus."

† It is said that the Mongolians in their career of conquest could move an army of 500,000 fifty miles a day, a speed out of the question with all the facilities of modern warfare.

A wondrous breed, whose famed descendants bore
The Moslem hosts that swept from off the earth
Thy mighty power, corrupt, declining Rome,
And with each other now alone contend
In speed, whose sons cast out, abused and starved,
Alone can save from raging whirlwind flames*
That all-devouring sweep our western plains;
Then stately elephants came next in line,
With measured step and gently swaying gait,
Covered with cloth of gold richly inwrought,
Each bearing in a howdah gaily decked
A fair competitor for beauty's prize,
With merry comrades and some sober friend;
The vina, bansuli, sitar and harp
Filling the air with sweetest melody,
While rippling laughter from each howdah rang,
And sweetest odors, as from op'ning flowers,
Breathed from their rich apparel as they passed.

And thus they circle round the maidan wide,
And as they pass along the people shout,
"Long live the king! long live our noble prince!"
To all which glad acclaims the prince responds
With heartfelt courtesy and royal grace.

When they had nearly reached the palace gate
On their return, the king drew to the right
With his attendants, while the prince with his
Drew to the left, reviewing all the line

---

* See Bret Harte's beautiful poem, "Sell Patchin," and also an article on the "Horses of the Plains," in *The Century*, January, 1889.

That passed again down to the judges' seat,
Under the king's pavilion near the lake.
The prince eagerly watched them as they passed,
Noting their brawny limbs and polished arms,
The pose and skill of every charioteer,
The parts and varied breed of every horse,
Aiding his comrades with his deeper skill.
But when the queens of beauty passed him by,
He was all smiles and gallantry and grace,
Until the last, Yasodhara, came near,
Whose laugh was clearest of the merry crowd,
Whose golden hair imprisoned sunlight seemed,
Whose cheek, blending the lily with the rose,
Spoke of more northern skies and Aryan blood,
Whose rich, not gaudy, robes exquisite taste
Had made to suit her so they seemed a part
Of her sweet self; whose manner, simple, free,
Not bold or shy, whose features — no one saw
Her features, for her soul covered her face
As with a veil of ever-moving life.
When she came near, and her bright eyes met his,
He seemed to start; his gallantry was gone,
And like an awkward boy he sat and gazed;
And her laugh too was hushed, and she passed on,
Passed out of sight but never out of mind.
The king and all his counselors saw this.
"Good king, our deer is struck," Asita said,
"If this love cure him not, nothing can cure."

BOOK II.

She passed along, and then the king and prince
With their attendants wheeled in line and moved
Down to the royal stand, each to his place.

The trumpets sound, and now the games begin.

But see the scornful curl of Culture's lip
At such low sports! Dyspeptic preachers hear
Harangue the sleepers on their sinfulness!
Hear grave philosophers, so limp and frail
They scarce can walk God's earth to breathe his air,
Talk of the waste of time! Short-sighted men!
God made the body just to fit the mind,
Each part exact, no scrimping and no waste —
Neglect the body and you cramp the soul.

First brawny wrestlers, shining from the bath,
Wary and watchful, quick with arm and eye,
After long play clinch close, arms twined, knees locked,

Each nerve and muscle strained, and stand as still
As if a bronze from Vulcan's fabled shop,
Or else by power of magic changed to stone
In that supremest moment, when a breath
Or feather's weight would tip the balanced scale;
And when they fall the shouts from hill to hill
Sound like the voices of the mighty deep,
As wave on wave breaks on the rock-bound shore.

Then boxers, eye to eye and foot to foot,
One arm at guard, the other raised to strike.

The hurlers of the quoit next stand in line,
Measure the distance with experienced eye,
Adjust the rings, swing them with growing speed,
Until at length on very tiptoe poised,
Like Mercury just lighted on the earth,
With mighty force they whirl them through the air.

And then the spearmen, having for a mark
A lion rampant, standing as in life,
So distant that it seemed but half life-size,
Each vital part marked with a little ring,
And when the spears were hurled, six trembling stood
Fixed in the beast, piercing each vital part,
Leaving the victory in even scale.
For these was set far off a lesser mark,
Until at length by chance, not lack of skill,
The victory so long in doubt was won.

And then again the people wildly shout,
The prince victor and nobly vanquished praised.

  Next runners, lithe and light, glide round the plain,
Whose flying feet like Mercury's seemed winged,
Their chests expanded, and their swinging arms
Like oars to guide and speed their rapid course;
And as they passed along the people cheered
Each well-known master of the manly art.

  Then archers, with broad chests and brawny arms
Such as the blacksmith's heavy hammer wields
With quick, hard blows that make the anvil ring
And myriad sparks from the hot iron fly;
A golden eagle on a screen their mark,
So distant that it seemed a sparrow's size —
" For," said the prince, " let not this joyful day
Give anguish to the smallest living thing."
They strain their bows until their muscles seem
Like knotted cords, the twelve strings twang at once,
And the ground trembles as at the swelling tones
Of mighty organs or the thunder's roll.
Two arrows pierce the eagle, while the rest
All pierce the screen. A second mark was set,
When lo! high up in air two lines of swans,
Having one leader, seek their northern nests,
Their white plumes shining in the noonday sun,
Calling each other in soft mellow notes.

Instant one of the people cries " A mark !"
Whereat the thousands shout "A mark ! a mark !"
One of the archers chose the leader, one the last.
Their arrows fly. The last swan left its mates
As if sore wounded, while the first came down
Like a great eagle swooping for its prey,
And fell before the prince, its strong wing pierced,
Its bright plumes darkened by its crimson blood.
Whereat the people shout, and shout again,
Until the hills repeat the mighty sound.
The prince gently but sadly raised the bird,
Stroked tenderly its plumes, calmed its wild fear,
And gave to one to care for and to cure.

And now the people for the chariot-race
Grow eager, while beneath the royal stand,
By folding doors hid from the public view,
The steeds, harnessed and ready, champ their bits
And paw the ground, impatient for the start.
The charioteers alert, with one strong hand
Hold high the reins, the other holds the lash.
Timour — a name that since has filled the world,
A Tartar chief, whose sons long after swept
As with destruction's broom fair India's plains—
With northern jargon calmed his eager steeds ;
Azim, from Cashmere's rugged lovely vale,
His prancing Babylonians firmly held ;
Channa, from Ganges' broad and sacred stream,
With bit and word checked his Nisæan three ;
While Devadatta, cousin to the prince,
Soothed his impatient Arabs with such terms

As fondest mothers to their children use :
"Atair, my pet ! Mira, my baby, hush !
Regil, my darling child, be still ! be still !"
With necks high arched, nostrils distended wide,
And eager gaze, they stood as those that saw
Some distant object in their desert home.

At length the gates open as of themselves,
When at the trumpet's sound the steeds dash forth
As by one spirit moved, under tight rein,
And neck and neck they thunder down the plain,
While rising dust-clouds chase the flying wheels.
But weight, not lack of nerve or spirit, tells ;
Azim and Channa urge their steeds in vain,
By Tartar and light Arab left behind
As the light galley leaves the man-of-war ;
They sweat and labor ere a mile is gained,
While their light rivals pass the royal stand
Fresh as at first, just warming to the race.

And now the real race at length begins,
A double race, such as the Romans loved.
Horses so matched in weight and strength and
    speed,
Drivers so matched in skill that as they pass
Azim and Channa seemed a single man.
Timour and Devadatta, side by side,
Wheel almost touching wheel, dash far ahead.

Azim and Channa, left so far behind,
No longer urge a race already lost.

The Babylonian and Nisæan steeds,
No longer pressed so far beyond their power,
With long and even strides sweep smoothly on,
Striking the earth as with a single blow,
Their hot breath rising in a single cloud.
Arab and Tartar with a longer stride
And lighter stroke skim lightly o'er the ground.
Watching the horses with a master's eye,
As Devadatta and Timour four times,
Azim and Channa thrice, swept by the stand,
The prince saw that another round would test,
Not overtax, their powers, and gave the sign,
When three loud trumpet-blasts to all proclaimed
That running one more round would end the race.
These ringing trumpet-calls that brought defeat
Or victory so near, startle and rouse.
The charioteers more ardent urge their steeds;
The steeds are with hot emulation fired;
The social multitude now cease to talk —
Even age stops short in stories often told;
Boys, downy-chinned, in rough-and-tumble sports
Like half-grown bears engaged, turn quick and look;
And blooming girls, with merry ringing laugh,
Romping in gentler games, watching meanwhile
With sly and sidelong look the rougher sports,
Turn eagerly to see the scene below;
While mothers for the time forget their babes,
And lovers who had sought out quiet nooks
To tell the tale that all the past has told
And coming times will tell, stand mute and gaze.

The home-stretch soon is reached, and Channa's three
By word and lash urged to their topmost speed,
The foaming Babylonians left behind,
While Devadatta and Timour draw near,
A whole round gained, Timour a length ahead.
But Devadatta loosens now his reins,
Chides his fleet pets, with lash swung high in air
Wounds their proud spirits, not their tender flesh.
With lion-bounds they pass the Tartar steeds,
That with hot rival rage and open mouths,
And flaming eyes, and fierce and angry cries,
Dash full at Regil's side, but dash in vain.
Fear adding speed, the Arabs sweep ahead.
Meanwhile the prince springs forward from his seat,
And all on tiptoe still and eager stand,
So that the rumbling of the chariot-wheels,
The tramp of flying feet and drivers' cries,
Alone the universal stillness break —
As when before the bursting of some fearful storm,
Birds, beasts and men stand mute with trembling awe,
While heaven's artillery and roaring winds
Are in the awful silence only heard.
But when the double victory is gained,
Drums, shells and trumpets mingle with the shouts
From hill to hill re-echoed and renewed —
As when, after the morning's threatening bow,
Dark, lurid, whirling clouds obscure the day,
And forked lightnings dart athwart the sky,
And angry winds roll up the boiling sea,

And thunder, raging winds and warring waves
Join in one mighty and earth-shaking roar.

   Thus end the games, and the procession forms,
The king and elders first, contestants next,
And last the prince : each victor laurel-crowned,
And after each his prize, while all were given
Some choice memorial of the happy day—
Cinctures to all athletes to gird the loins
And falling just below the knee, the belt
Of stoutest leather, joined with silver clasps,
The skirt of softest wool or finest silk,
Adorned with needlework and decked with gems,
Such as the modest Aryans always wore
In games intended for the public view,
Before the Greeks became degenerate,
And savage Rome compelled those noble men
Whose only crime was love of liberty,
By discipline and numbers overwhelmed,
Bravely defending children, wife and home,
Naked to fight each other or wild beasts,
And called this brutal savagery high sport
For them and for their proud degenerate dames,
Of whom few were what Cæsar's wife should be.
The athletes' prizes all were rich and rare,
Some costly emblem of their several arts.
The archers' prizes all were bows ; the first
Made from the horns of a great mountain-goat
That long had ranged the Himalayan heights,
Till some bold hunter climbed his giddy cliffs
And brought his unsuspecting victim down.

His lofty horns the bowsmith root to root
Had firmly joined, and polished bright,
And tipped with finest gold, and made a bow
Worthy of Sinhahamu's* mighty arm.
The other prizes, bows of lesser strength
But better suited to their weaker arms.
A chariot, the charioteers' first prize,†
Its slender hubs made strong with brazen bands,
The spokes of whitest ivory polished bright,
The fellies ebony, with tires of bronze,
Each axle's end a brazen tiger's head,
The body woven of slender bamboo shoots
Intwined with silver wire and decked with gold.
A mare and colt of the victorious breed
The second prize, more worth in Timour's eyes
Than forty chariots, though each were made
Of ebony or ivory or gold,
And all the laurel India ever grew.
The third, a tunic of soft Cashmere wool,
On which, by skillful needles deftly wrought,
The race itself as if in life stood forth.
The fourth, a belt to gird the laggard's loins
And whip to stimulate his laggard steeds.

---

* Sinhabamu was an ancestor, said to be the grandfather, of our prince, whose bow, like that of Ulysses, no one else could bend. See notes 24 and 25 to Book Second of Arnold's "Light of Asia."

† Any one who has read that remarkable work, "Ben Hur," and every one who has not should, will recognize my obligations to General Wallace.

And thus arrayed they moved once round the
    course,
Then to the palace, as a fitter place
For beauty's contest than the open plain;
The singers chanting a triumphal hymn,
While many instruments, deep toned and shrill,
And all the multitude, the chorus swell.

This day his mission ceased to press the prince,
And he forgot the sorrows of the world,
So deep and earnest seemed the general joy.
Even those with grinning skeletons at home
In secret closets locked from public view,
And care and sorrow rankling at their hearts,
Joined in the general laugh and swelled the shouts,
And seemed full happy though they only seemed.
But through the games, while all was noisy mirth,
He felt a new, strange feeling at his heart,
And ever and anon he stole a glance
At beauty's rose-embowered hiding-place,
To catch a glimpse of those two laughing eyes,
So penetrating yet so soft and mild.
And at the royal banquet spread for all
It chanced Yasodhara sat next the prince —
An accident by older heads designed —
And the few words that such constraint allowed
Were music to his ears and touched his heart;
And when her eyes met his her rosy blush
Told what her maiden modesty would hide.
And at the dance, when her soft hands touched his
The music seemed to quicken, time to speed;

But when she bowed and passed to other hands,
Winding the mystic measure of the dance,*
The music seemed to slacken, time to halt,
Or drag his limping moments lingering on.
At length, after the dance, the beauties passed
Before the prince, and each received her prize,
So rich and rare that each thought hers the first,
A treasure to be kept and shown with pride,
And handed down to children yet unborn.
But when Yasodhara before him stood,
The prizes all were gone.; but from his neck
He took a golden chain thick set with gems,
And clasped it round her slender waist, and said:
"Take this, and keep it for the giver's sake."

And from the prince they passed before the king.
The proud and stately he would greet with grace,
The timid cheer with kind and gracious words.
But when Yasodhara bowed low and passed,
He started, and his color went and came
As if oppressed with sudden inward pain.
Asita, oldest of his counselors,
Sprang to his side and asked: "What ails the
    king?"
"Nothing, my friend, nothing," the king replied,
"But the sharp probing of an ancient wound.
You know how my sweet queen was loved of all —

---

*One may be satisfied with the antiquity of the dance, practically as we have it, from lines 187-8, Book VI, of the Odyssey:
  "Joyful they see applauding princes gaze
    When stately in the dance they swim the harmonious maze."

But how her life was woven into mine,
Filling my inmost soul, none e'er can know.
My bitter anguish words can never tell,
As that sweet life was gently breathed away.
Time only strengthens this enduring love,
And she seems nearer me as I grow old.
Often in stillest night's most silent hour,
When the sly nibbling of a timid mouse
In the deep stillness sounds almost as loud
As builders' hammers in the busy day,
My Maya as in life stands by my side,
A halo round her head, as she would say:
'A little while, and you shall have your own.'
Often in deepest sleep she seems to steal
Into that inmost chamber of my soul
Vacant for her, and nestle to my heart,
Breathing a peace my waking hours know not.
And when I wake, and turn to clasp my love
My sinking heart finds but her vacant place.
Since that sad day that stole her from my arms
I've seen a generation of sweet girls
Grow up to womanhood, but none like her!
But that bright vision that just flitted by
Seemed so like her it made me cringe and start.
O dear Asita, little worth is life,
With all its tears and partings, woes and pains,
If when its short and fitful fever ends
There is no after-life, where death and pain,
And sundered ties, and crushed and bleeding hearts,
And sad and last farewells are never known."

Such was the old and such the new-born love;
The new quick bursting into sudden flame,
Warming the soul to active consciousness
That man alone is but a severed part
Of one full, rounded, perfect, living whole;
The old a steady but undying flame,
A living longing for the loved and lost;
But each a real hunger of the soul
For what gave paradise its highest bliss,
And what in this poor fallen world of ours
Gives glimpses of its high and happy life.

O love! how beautiful! how pure! how sweet!
Life of the angels that surround God's throne!
But when corrupt, Pandora's box itself,
Whence spring all human ills and woes and crimes,
The very fire that lights the flames of hell.

The festival is past. The crowds have gone,
The diligent to their accustomed round
Of works and days, works to each day assigned,
The thoughtless and the thriftless multitude
To meet their tasks haphazard as they come,
But all the same old story to repeat
Of cares and sorrows sweetened by some joys.

Three days the sweet Yasodhara remained,
For her long journey taking needful rest.
But when the rosy dawn next tinged the east
And lit the mountain-tops and filled the park
With a great burst of rich and varied song.

The good old king bade the sweet girl farewell,
Imprinting on her brow a loving kiss,
While welling up from tender memories
Big tear-drops trickled down his furrowed cheeks.
And as her train, escorted by the prince
And noble youth, wound slowly down the hill,
The rising sun with glory gilds the city
That like a diadem circled its brow,
While giant shadows stretch across the plain;
And when they reach the plain they halt for rest
Deep in a garden's cooling shade, where flowers
That fill the air with grateful fragrance hang
By ripening fruits, and where all seems at rest
Save two young hearts and tiny tireless birds
That dart from flower to flower to suck their sweets,
And even the brook that babbled down the hill
Now murmurs dreamily as if asleep.
Sweet spot! sweet hour! how quick its moments fly!
How soon the cooling winds and sinking sun
And bustling stir of preparation tells
'Tis time for her to go; and when they part,
The gentle pressure of the hand, one kiss —
A kiss not given yet not resisted — tells
A tale of love that words are poor to tell.
And when she goes how lonely seems her way
  Through groves, through fields, through busy haunts of men;
And as he climbs the hill and often stops
To watch her lessening train until at length
Her elephant seems but a moving speck.
Proud Kantaka, pawing and neighing, asks

As plain as men could ever ask in words:
"What makes my master choose this laggard
    pace?"

At length she climbs those rocky, rugged hills
That guarded well the loveliest spot on earth
Until the Moguls centuries after came,
Like swarms of locusts swept before the wind,
Or ravening wolves, to conquer fair Cashmere.*
And when she reached the top, before her lay,
As on a map spread out, her native land,
By lofty mountains walled on every side,
From winds, from wars, and from the world shut
    out ;
The same great snow-capped mountains north and
    east
In silent, glittering, awful grandeur stand,
And west the same bold, rugged, cliff-crowned hills
That filled her eyes with wonder when a child.
Below the snow a belt of deepest green ;
Below this belt of green great rolling hills,
Checkered with orchards, vineyards, pastures,
    fields,
The vale beneath peaceful as sleeping babe,
The city nestling round the shining lake,
And near the park and palace, her sweet home.

---

* I am aware I place Kapilavastu nearer the Vale of Cashmere than most, but as two such writers as Beal and Rhys Davids differ 30 yojanas or 180 miles in its location, and as no remains have yet been identified at all corresponding to the grandeur of the ancient city as described by all Buddhist writers, I felt free to indulge my fancy. Perhaps these ruins may yet be found by some chance traveler in some unexplored jungle.

O noble, peaceful, beautiful Cashmere!
Well named the garden of eternal spring!
But yet, with home and all its joys so near,
She often turned and strained her eager eyes
To catch one parting glimpse of that sweet spot
Where more than half of her young heart was left.

At length their horns, whose mocking echoes
Rolled from hill to hill, were answered from below,
While from the park a gay procession comes,
Increasing as it moves, to welcome her,
Light of the palace, the people's idol, home.

The prince's thoughts by day and dreams by night
Meanwhile were filled with sweet Yasodhara,
And this bright vision ever hovering near
Hid from his eyes those grim and ghastly forms,
Night-loving and light-shunning brood of sin,
That ever haunt poor fallen human lives,
And from the darkened corners of the soul
Are quick to sting each pleasure with sharp pain,
To pour some bitter in life's sweetest cup,
And shadow with despair its brightest hopes —
Made him forget how sorrow fills the world,
How strength is used to crush and not to raise,
How creeds are bandages to blind men's eyes,
Lest they should see and walk in duty's path
That leads to peace on earth and joy in heaven,
And even made him for the time forget
His noble mission to restore and save.

He sought her for his bride, but waited long,
For princes cannot wed like common folk —
Friends called, a feast prepared, some bridal gifts,
Some tears at parting and some solemn vows,
Rice scattered, slippers thrown with noisy mirth,
And common folk are joined till death shall part.
Till death shall part! O faithless, cruel thought!
Death ne'er shall part souls joined by holy love,
Who through life's trials, joys and cares
Have to each other clung, faithful till death,
Tender and true in sickness and in health,
Bearing each other's burdens, sharing griefs,
Lightening each care and heightening every joy.
Such life is but a transient honeymoon,
A feeble foretaste of eternal joys.
But princes when they love, though all approve,
Must wait on councils, embassies and forms.
But how the coach of state lumbers and lags
With messages of love whose own light wings
Glide through all bars, outstrip all fleetest things —
No bird so light, no thought so fleet as they.

But while the prince chafed at the long delay,
The sweet Yasodhara began to feel
The bitter pangs of unrequited love.
But her young hands, busy with others' wants,
And her young heart, busy with others' woes,
With acts of kindness filled the lagging hours,
Best of all medicines for aching hearts.
Yet often she would seek a quiet nook
Deep in the park, where giant trees cross arms,

Making high gothic arches, and a shade
That noonday's fiercest rays could scarcely pierce,
And there alone with her sad heart communed:
"Yes! I have kept it for the giver's sake,
But he has quite forgot his love, his gift, and me.
How bright these jewels seemed warmed by his love,
But now how dull, how icy and how dead!"
But soon the soft-eyed antelopes and fawns
And fleet gazelles came near and licked her hands;
And birds of every rich and varied plume
Gathered around and filled the air with song;
And even timid pheasants brought their broods,
For her sweet loving life had here restored
The peace and harmony of paradise;
And as they shared her bounty she was soothed
By their mute confidence and perfect trust.

But though time seems to lag, yet still it moves,
Resistless as the ocean's swelling tide,
Bearing its mighty freight of human lives
With all their joys and sorrows, hopes and fears,
Onward, forever onward, to life's goal.
At length the embassy is sent, and now,
Just as the last faint rays of rosy light
Fade from the topmost Himalayan peaks,
And tired nature sinks to quiet rest,
A horseman dashes through the silent streets
Bearing the waiting prince the welcome word
That one short journey of a single day
Divides him from the sweet Yasodhara;
And light-winged rumor spreads the joyful news,

And ere the dawn had danced from mountain-top
O'er hill and vale and plain to the sweet notes
Of nature's rich and varied orchestra,
And dried the pearly tears that night had wept,
The prince led forth his train to meet his bride,
Wondering that Kantaka, always so free,
So eager and so fleet, should seem to lag.
And in that fragrant garden's cooling shade,
Where they had parted, now again they meet,
And there we leave them reverently alone,
For art can never paint nor words describe
The peace and rest and rapture of that scene.

   Meanwhile the city rings with busy stir.
The streets are swept and sprinkled with perfumes,
And when the evening shades had veiled the earth,
And heaven's blue vault was set with myriad stars,
The promised signal from the watchtower sounds,
And myriad lamps shine from each house and tree,
And merry children strew their way with flowers,
And all come forth to greet Siddartha's bride,
And welcome her, their second Maya, home.
And at the palace gate the good old king
Receives her with such loving tenderness,
As fondest mother, sick with hope deferred,
Waiting and watching for an absent child,
At length receives him in her open arms.

BOOK III.

And now his cup with every blessing filled
Full to the brim, to overflowing full,
What more has life to give or heart to wish?
Stately in form, with every princely grace,
A very master of all manly arts,
His gentle manners making all his friends,
His young blood bounding on in healthful flow,
His broad domains rich in all earth can yield,
Guarded by nature and his people's love,
And now that deepest of all wants supplied,
The want of one to share each inmost thought,
Whose sympathy can soothe each inmost smart,
Whose presence, care and loving touch can make
The palace or the humblest cottage home,
His life seemed rounded, perfect, full, complete.
And they were happy as the days glide on,
And when at night, locked in each other's arms,
They sink to rest, heart beating close to heart,
Their thoughts all innocence and trust and love,
It almost seemed as if remorseless Time
Had backward rolled his tide, and brought again
The golden age, with all its peace and joy,

And our first parents, ere the tempter came,
Were taking sweet repose in paradise.
But as one night they slept, a troubled dream
Disturbed the prince. He dreamed he saw one come,
As young and fair as sweet Yasodhara,
But clad in widow's weeds, and in her arms
A lifeless child, crying: "Most mighty prince!
O bring me back my husband and my child!"
But he could only say "Alas! poor soul!"
And started out of sleep he cried "Alas!"
Which waked the sweet Yasodhara, who asked,
"What ails my love?" "Only a troubled dream,"
The prince replied, but still she felt him tremble,
And kissed and stroked his troubled brow,
And soothed him into quiet sleep again.
And then once more he dreamed—a pleasing dream.
He dreamed he heard strange music, soft and sweet;
He only caught its burden: "Peace, be still!"
And then he thought he saw far off a light,
And there a place where all was peace and rest,
And waking sighed to find it all a dream.

One day this happy couple, side by side,
Rode forth alone, Yasodhara unveiled —
"For why," said she, "should those whose thoughts are pure
Like guilty things hide from their fellow-men?"—
Rode through the crowded streets, their only guard
The people's love, strongest and best of guards;
For many arms would spring to their defense,
While some grim tyrant, at whose stern command

A million swords would from their scabbards leap,
Cringes in terror behind bolts and bars,
Starts at each sound, and fears some hidden mine
May into atoms blow his stately towers,
Or that some hand unseen may strike him down,
And thinks that poison lurks in every cup,
While thousands are in loathsome dungeons thrust
Or pine in exile for a look or word.
And as they pass along from street to street
A sea of happy faces lines their way,
Their joyful greetings answered by the prince.
No face once seen, no name once heard, forgot,
While sweet Yasodhara was wreathed in smiles,
The kind expression of her gentle heart,
When from a little cottage by the way,
The people making room for him to pass,
There came an aged man, so very old
That time had ceased to register his years;
His step was firm, his eye, though faded, mild,
And childhood's sweet expression on his face.
The prince stopped short before him, bending low,
And gently asked: " What would my father have?
Speak freely—what I can, I freely give."
"Most noble prince, I need no charity,
For my kind neighbors give me all unasked,
And my poor cottage where my fathers dwelt,
And where my children and their mother died,
Is kept as clean as when sweet Gunga lived;
And young and old cheer up my lonely hours,
And ask me much of other times and men.
For when your father's father was a child,

I was a man, as young and strong as you,
And my sweet Gunga your companion's age.
But O the mystery of life explain!
Why are we born to tread this little round,
To live, to love, to suffer, sorrow, die?
Why do the young like field-flowers bloom to fade?
Why are the strong like the mown grass cut down?
Why am I left as if by death forgot,
Left here alone, a leafless, fruitless trunk?
Is death the end, or what comes after death?
Often when deepest sleep shuts out the world,
The dead still seem to live, while life fades out;
And when I sit alone and long for light
The veil seems lifted, and I seem to see
A world of life and light and peace and rest,
No sickness, sin or sorrow, pain or death,
No helpless infancy or hopeless age.
But we poor Sudras cannot understand —
Yet from my earliest memory I've heard
That from this hill one day should burst a light,
Not for the Brahmans only, but for all.
And when you were a child I saw a sage
Bow down before you, calling you that light.
O noble, mighty prince! let your light shine,
That men no longer grope in dark despair!"

He spoke, and sank exhausted on the ground.
They gently raised him, but his life was fled.
The prince gave one a well-filled purse and said:
" Let his pile neither lack for sandal-wood
Or any emblem of a life well spent."

And when fit time had passed they bore him thence
And laid him on that couch where all sleep well,
Half hid in flowers by loving children brought,
A smile still lingering on his still, cold lips,
As if they just had tasted Gunga's kiss,
Soon to be kissed by eager whirling flames.

   Just then two stately Brahmans proudly passed —
Passed on the other side, gathering their robes
To shun pollution from the common touch,
And passing said : " The prince with Sudras talks
As friend to friend — but wisdom comes with years."

Silent and thoughtful then they homeward turned,
The prince deep musing on the old man's words :
"'The veil is lifted, and I seem to see
A world of life and light and peace and rest.'
O if that veil would only lift for me
The mystery of life would be explained."
As they passed on through unfrequented streets,
Seeking to shun the busy, thoughtless throng,
Those other words like duty's bugle-call
Still ringing in his ears : " Let your light shine,
That men no longer grope in dark despair " —
The old sad thoughts, long checked by passing joys,
Rolling and surging, swept his troubled soul —
As pent-up waters, having burst their dams,
Sweep down the valleys and o'erwhelm the plains.

   Just then an aged, angry voice cried out :
" O help ! they've stolen my jewels and my gold !"

And from a wretched hovel by the way
An old man came, hated and shunned by all,
Whose life was spent in hoarding unused gold,
Grinding the poor, devouring widows' homes;
Ill fed, ill clad, from eagerness to save,
His sunken eyes glittering with rage and greed.
And when the prince enquired what troubled him:
"Trouble enough," he said, "my sons have fled
Because I would not waste in dainty fare
And rich apparel all my life has saved,
And taken all my jewels, all my gold.
Would that they both lay dead before my face!
O precious jewels! O beloved gold!"
The prince, helpless to soothe, hopeless to cure
This rust and canker of the soul, passed on,
His heart with all-embracing pity filled.
"O deepening mystery of life!" he cried,
"Why do such souls in human bodies dwell—
Fitter for ravening wolves or greedy swine!
Just at death's door cursing his flesh and blood
For thievish greed inherited from him.
Is this old age, or swinish greed grown old?
O how unlike that other life just fled!
His youth's companions, wife and children, dead,
Yet filled with love for all, by all beloved,
With his whole heart yearning for others' good,
With his last breath bewailing others' woes."
"My best beloved," said sweet Yasodhara,
Her bright eyes filled with sympathetic tears,
Her whole soul yearning for his inward peace,
"Brood not too much on life's dark mystery—

Behind the darkest clouds the sun still shines."
"But," said the prince, "the many blindly grope
In sorrow, fear and ignorance profound,
While their proud teachers, with their heads erect,
Stalk boldly on, blind leaders of the blind.
Come care, come fasting, woe and pain for me,
And even exile from my own sweet home,
All would I welcome could I give them light."
"But would you leave your home, leave me, leave all,
And even leave our unborn pledge of love,
The living blending of our inmost souls,
That now within me stirs to bid you pause?"
"Only for love of you and him and all!
O hard necessity! O bitter cup!
But would you have me like a coward shun
The path of duty, though beset with thorns —
Thorns that must pierce your tender feet and mine?"
Piercing the question as the sharpest sword;
Their love, their joys, tempted to say him nay.
But soon she conquered all and calmly said:
"My love, my life, where duty plainly calls
I bid you go, though my poor heart must bleed,
And though my eyes weep bitter scalding tears."

Their hearts too full for words, too full for tears,
Gently he pressed her hand and they passed home;
And in the presence of this dark unknown
A deep and all-pervading tenderness
Guides every act and tempers every tone —
As in the chamber of the sick and loved
The step is light, the voice is soft and low.

But soon their days with varied duties filled,
Their nights with sweet repose, glide smoothly on,
Until this shadow seems to lift and fade—
As when the sun bursts through the passing storm,
Gilding the glittering raindrops as they fall,
And paints the bow of hope on passing clouds.
Yet still the old sad thoughts sometimes return,
The burden of a duty unperformed,
The earnest yearning for a clearer light.
The thought that hour by hour and day by day
The helpless multitudes grope blindly on,
Clouded his joys and often banished sleep.

  One day in this sad mood he thought to see
His people as they are in daily life,
And not in holiday attire to meet their prince.
In merchant's dress, his charioteer his clerk,
The prince and Channa passed unknown, and saw
The crowded streets alive with busy hum,
Traders cross-legged, with their varied wares,
The wordy war to cheapen or enhance,
One rushing on to clear the streets for wains
With huge stone wheels, by slow strong oxen
    drawn;
Palanquin-bearers droning out "Hu, hu, ho, ho,"
While keeping step and praising him they bear;
The housewives from the fountain water bring
In balanced water-jars, their black-eyed babes
Athwart their hips, their busy tongues meanwhile
Engaged in gossip of the little things
That make the daily round of life to them;

The skillful weaver at his clumsy loom;
The miller at his millstones grinding meal;
The armorer, linking his shirts of mail;
The money-changer at his heartless trade;
The gaping, eager crowd gathered to watch
Snake-charmers, that can make their deadly charge
Dance harmless to the drone of beaded gourds;
Sword-players, keeping many knives in air;
Jugglers, and those that dance on ropes swung high:
And all this varied work and busy idleness
As in a panorama passing by.

   While they were passing through these varied scenes,
The prince, whose ears were tuned to life's sad notes,
Whose eyes were quick to catch its deepest shades,
Found sorrow, pain and want, disease and death,
Were woven in its very warp and woof.
A tiger, springing from a sheltering bush,
Had snatched a merchant's comrade from his side;
A deadly cobra, hidden by the path,
Had stung to death a widow's only son;
A breath of jungle-wind a youth's blood chilled,
Or filled a strong man's bones with piercing pain;
A household widowed by a careless step;
The quick cross-lightning from an angry cloud
Struck down a bridegroom bringing home his bride—
All this and more he heard, and much he saw:

A young man, stricken in life's early prime,
Shuffled along, dragging one palsied limb,
While one limp arm hung useless by his side ;
A dwarf sold little knickknacks by the way,
His body scarcely in the human form,
To which long arms and legs seemed loosely hung,
His noble head thrust forward on his breast,
Whose pale, sad face as plainly told as words
That life had neither health nor hope for him ;
An old man tottering from a hovel came,
Frail, haggard, palsied, leaning on a staff,
Whose eyes, dull, glazed and meaningless, proclaim
The body lingers when the mind has fled ;
One seized with sudden hot distemper of the blood,
Writhing with anguish, by the wayside sunk,
The purple plague-spot on his pallid cheek,
Cold drops of perspiration on his brow,
With wildly rolling eyes and livid lips,
Gasping for breath and feebly asking help —
But ere the prince could aid, death gave relief.

At length they passed the city's outer gate
And down a stream, now spread in shining pools,
Now leaping in cascades, now dashing on,
A line of foam along its rocky bed,
Bordered by giant trees with densest shade.
Here, day by day, the city bring their dead ;
Here, day by day, they build the funeral-piles ;
Here lamentations daily fill the air ;
Here hissing flames each day taste human flesh,

And friendly watchmen guard the smoldering pile
Till friends can cull the relics from the dust.
And here, just finished, rose a noble pile
By stately Brahmans for a Brahman built
Of fragrant woods, and drenched with fragrant oils,
Loading the air with every sweet perfume
That India's forests or her fields can yield ;
Above, a couch of sacred cusa-grass,
On which no dreams disturb the sleeper's rest.
And now the sound of music reaches them,
Far off at first, solemn and sad and slow,
Rising and swelling as it nearer comes,
Until a long procession comes in view,
Four Brahmans first, bearing in bowls the fire
No more to burn on one deserted hearth.
Then stately Brahmans on their shoulders bore
A noble brother of their sacred caste,
In manhood's bloom and early prime cut down.
Then Brahman youth, bearing a little child
Half hid in flowers, and as in seeming sleep.
Then other Brahmans in a litter bore
One young and fair, in early womanhood,
Her youthful beauty joined with matron grace,
In bridal dress adorned with costly gems —
The very face the prince had dreaming seen,
The very child she carried in her arms.
Then many more, uncovered, four by four,
The aged first, then those in manhood's prime,
And then the young with many acolytes
Chanting in unison their sacred hymns,

Accompanied by many instruments,
Both wind and string, in solemn symphony;
And at respectful distance other castes,
Afraid to touch a Brahman's sacred robes
Or even mingle with his grief their tears.
And when they reached the fragrant funeral-pile,
Weeping they placed their dead on their last couch,
The child within its father's nerveless arms;
And when all funeral rites had been performed,
The widow circled thrice the funeral-pile,
Distributing her gifts with lavish hand,
Bidding her friends a long and last farewell —
Then stopped, and raised her tearless eyes and said:
" Farewell, a long farewell, to life and friends!
Farewell! O earth and air and sacred sun!
Nanda, my lord, Udra, my child, I come!"
Then pale but calm, with fixed ecstatic gaze
And steady steps she mounts the funeral-pile,
Crying, " They beckon me! I come! I come!"
Then sunk as if the silver cord were loosed
As still as death upon her silent dead.
Instant the flames from the four corners leaped,
Mingling in one devouring, eager blaze.
No groan, no cry, only the crackling flames,
The wailing notes of many instruments,
And solemn chant by many voices raised,
" Perfect is she who follows thus her lord."
O dark and cruel creeds, O perfect love,
Fitter for heaven than this sad world of ours!

More than enough the prince had seen and heard.

Bowed by the grievous burdens others bore,
Feeling for others' sorrows as his own,
Tears of divinest pity filled his eyes
And deep and all-embracing love his heart.
Home he returned, no more to find its rest.

   But soon a light shines in that troubled house—
A son is born to sweet Yasodhara.
Their eyes saw not, neither do ours, that sun
Whose light is wisdom and whose heat is love,
Sending through nature waves of living light,
Giving its life to everything that lives,
Which through the innocence of little ones
As through wide-open windows sends his rays
To light the darkest, warm the coldest heart.
Sweet infancy! life's solace and its rest,
Driving away the loneliness of age,
Wreathing in smiles the wrinkled brow of care,
Nectar to joyful, balm to troubled hearts.
Joyful once more is King Suddhodana;
A placid joy beams from that mother's face;
Joy lit the palace, flew from street to street,
And from the city over hill and plain;
Joy filled the prince's agitated soul —
He felt a power, from whence he could not tell,
Drawing away, he knew not where it led.
He knew the dreaded separation near,
Yet half its pain and bitterness was passed.
He need not leave his loved ones comfortless —
His loving people still would have their prince,
The king in young Rahula have his son,

And sweet Yasodhara, his very life,
Would have that nearest, dearest comforter
To soothe her cares and drive away her tears.*

But now strange dreams disturb the good old king—
Dreams starting him in terror from his sleep,
Yet seeming prophecies of coming good.
He dreamed he saw the flag his fathers loved
In tatters torn and trailing in the dust,
But in its place another glorious flag,
Whose silken folds seemed woven thick with gems
That as it waved glittered with dazzling light.
He dreamed he saw proud embassies from far
Bringing the crowns and scepters of the earth,
Bowing in reverence before the prince,
Humbly entreating him to be their king —
From whom he fled in haste as if in fear.
Then dreamed he saw his son in tattered robes
Begging from Sudras for his daily bread.
Again, he dreamed he saw the ancient tower
Where he in worship had so often knelt,
Rising and shining clothed with living light,
And on its top the prince, beaming with love,
Scattering with lavish hand the richest gems
On eager crowds that caught them as they fell.
But soon it vanished, and he saw a hill,
Rugged and bleak, cliff crowned and bald and bare,

---

* In the "Light of Asia" the prince is made to leave his young wife before the birth of their son, saying:
"Whom, if I wait to bless, my heart will fail,"
—a piece of cowardice hardly consistent with my conception of that brave and self-denying character.

And there he saw the prince, kneeling alone,
Wasted with cruel fastings till his bones
Clave to his skin, and in his sunken eyes
With fitful flicker gleamed the lamp of life
Until they closed, and on the ground he sank,
As if in death or in a deadly swoon;
And then the hill sank to a spreading plain,
Stretching beyond the keenest vision's ken,
Covered with multitudes as numberless
As ocean's sands or autumn's forest leaves;
And mounted on a giant elephant,
White as the snows on Himalaya's peaks,
The prince rode through their midst in royal state,
And as he moved along he heard a shout,
Rising and swelling, like the mighty voice
Of many waters breaking on the shore:
"All hail! great Chakravartin, king of kings!
Hail! king of righteousness! Hail! prince of
　　peace!"

　Strange dreams! Where is their birthplace —
　　where their home?
Lighter than foam upon the crested wave,
Fleeter than shadows of the passing cloud,
They are of such fantastic substance made
That quick as thought they change their fickle
　　forms —
Now grander than the waking vision views,
Now stranger than the wildest fancy feigns,
And now so grim and terrible they start
The hardened conscience from its guilty sleep.

In troops they come, trooping they fly away,
Waved into being by the magic wand
Of some deep purpose of the inmost soul,
Some hidden joy or sorrow, guilt or fear —
Or better, as the wise of old believed,
Called into being by some heavenly guest
To soothe, to warn, instruct or terrify.

   Strange dreams by night and troubled thoughts
      by day
Disturb the prince and banish quiet sleep.
He dreamed that darkness, visible and dense,
Shrouded the heavens and brooded o'er the earth,
Whose rayless, formless, vacant nothingness
Curdled his blood and made his eyeballs ache;
When suddenly from out this empty void
A cloud, shining with golden light, was borne
By gentle winds, loaded with sweet perfumes,
Sweeter than springtime on this earth can yield.
The cloud passed just above him, and he saw
Myriads of cherub faces looking down,
Sweet as Rahula, freed from earthly stain;
Such faces mortal brush could never paint —
Enraptured Raphael ne'er such faces saw.
But still the outer darkness hovered near,
And ever and anon a bony hand
Darts out to snatch some cherub face away.
Then dreamed he saw a broad and pleasant land,
With cities, gardens, groves and fruitful fields,
Where bee-fed flowers half hide the ripening fruits,
And spicy breezes stir the trembling leaves,

And many birds make sweetest melody,
But bordered by a valley black as night,
That ever vomits from its sunless depths
Great whirling clouds of suffocating smoke,
Blacker than hide the burning Ætna's head,
Blacker than over Lake Avernus hung;
No bird could fly above its fatal fumes;
Eagles, on tireless pinions upward borne,
In widening circles rising toward the sun,
Venturing too near its exhalations, fall,
As sinks the plummet in the silent sea;
And lions, springing on their antlered prey,
Drop still and lifeless on its deadly brink;
Only the jackal's dismal howl is heard
To break its stillness and eternal sleep.
He was borne forward to the very verge
Of this dark valley, by some power unseen.
A wind that pierced his marrow parts the clouds,
And far within, below he saw a sight
That stood his hair on end, beaded his brow
With icy drops, and made his blood run cold:
He saw a lofty throne, blacker than jet,
But shining with a strange and baleful light
That made him shade his blinded, dazzled eyes.
And seated on that throne a ghastly form
That seemed a giant human skeleton,
But yet in motion terrible and quick
As lightning, killing ere the thunders roll;
His fleshless skull had on a seeming crown,
While from his sunken sockets glared his eyes
Like coals of fire or eyes of basilisk,

And from his bony hand each instant flew
Unerring darts that flew to pierce and kill,
Piercing the infant in its mother's arms,
The mother when she feels her first-born's breath,
Piercing the father in his happy home,
Piercing the lover tasting love's first kiss,
Piercing the vanquished when his banners fall,
Piercing the victor 'mid triumphant shouts,
Piercing the mighty monarch on his throne;
While from a towering cypress growing near
Every disease to which frail flesh is heir
Like ravening vultures watch each arrow's flight,
And quick as thought glide off on raven's wings
To bring the wounded, writhing victim in —
As well-trained hunters mark their master's aim,
Then fly to bring the wounded quarry home.
Meanwhile a stifling stench rose from below —
As from a battle-field where nations met
And fiery ranks of living valor fought,
Now food for vultures, moldering cold and low —
And bleaching bones were scattered everywhere.

Startled he wakes and rises from his couch.
The lamps shine down with soft and mellow light.
The fair Yasodhara still lay in sleep,
But not in quiet sleep. Her bosom heaved
As if a sigh were seeking to escape;
Her brows were knit as if in pain or fear,
And tears were stealing from her close-shut lids.
But sweet Rahula slept, and sleeping smiled
As if he too those cherub faces saw.

In haste alone he noiselessly stole forth
To wander in the park, and cool his brow
And calm his burdened, agitated soul.
The night had reached that hour preceding dawn
When nature seems in solemn silence hushed,
Awed by the glories of the coming day.
The moon hung low above the western plains;
Unnumbered stars with double brightness shine,
And half-transparent mists the landscape veil,
Through which the mountains in dim grandeur
    rise.
Silent, alone he crossed the maidan wide
Where first he saw the sweet Yasodhara,
Where joyful multitudes so often met,
Now still as that dark valley of his dream.
He passed the lake, mirror of heaven's high vault,
Whose ruffled waters ripple on the shore,
Stirred by cool breezes from the snow-capped peaks;
And heedless of his way passed on and up,
Through giant cedars and the lofty pines,
Over a leafy carpet, velvet soft,
While solemn voices from their branches sound,
Strangely in unison with his sad soul;
And on and up until he reached a spot
Above the trees, above the mist-wrapped world,
Where opening chasms yawned on every side.
Perforce he stopped; and, roused from revery,
Gazed on the dark and silent world below.
The moon had sunk from sight, the stars grew dim,
And densest darkness veiled the sleeping world,
When suddenly bright beams of rosy light

Shot up the east; the highest mountain-top
Glittered as if both land and sea had joined
Their richest jewels and most costly gems
To make its crown; from mountain-peak to peak
The brightness spread, and darkness slunk away,
Until between two giant mountain-tops
Glittered a wedge of gold; the hills were tinged,
And soon the sun flooded the world with light
As when the darkness heard that first command:
"Let there be light!" and light from chaos shone.
Raptured he gazed upon the glorious scene.
"And can it be," he said, "with floods of light
Filling the blue and boundless vault above,
Bathing in brightness mountain, hill and plain,
Sending its rays to ocean's hidden depths,
With light for bird and beast and creeping thing,
Light for all eyes, oceans of light to spare,
That man alone from outer darkness comes,
Gropes blindly on his brief and restless round,
And then in starless darkness disappears?
There must be light, fountains of living light,
For which my thirsty spirit pining pants
As pants the hunted hart for water-brooks —
Another sun, lighting a better world,
Where weary souls may find a welcome rest.
Gladly I'd climb yon giddy mountain-heights,
Or gladly take the morning's wings and fly
To earth's remotest bounds, if light were there.
Welcome to me the hermit's lonely cell,
And welcome dangers, labors, fastings, pains —
All would be welcome could I bring the light

To myriads now in hopeless darkness sunk.
Farewell to kingdom, comforts, home and friends !
All will I leave to seek this glorious light."
The die is cast, the victory is gained.
Though love of people, parent, wife and child,
Half selfish, half divine, may bid him pause,
A higher love, unselfish, all divine,
For them and every soul, bade him go forth
To seek for light, and seek till light be found.
Home he returned, now strong to say farewell.

    Meanwhile the sweet Yasodhara still slept,
And dreamed she saw Siddartha's empty couch.
She dreamed she saw him flying far away,
And when she called to him he answered not,
But only stopped his ears and faster flew
Until he seemed a speck, and then was gone.
And then she heard a mighty voice cry out:
"The time has come — his glory shall appear !"
Waked by that voice, she found his empty couch,
Siddartha gone, and with him every joy ;
But not all joy, for there Rahula lay,
With great wide-open eyes and cherub smile,
Watching the lights that flickered on the wall.
Caught in her arms she pressed him to her heart
To still its tumult and to ease its pain.

    But now that step she knew so well is heard.
Siddartha comes, filled with unselfish love
Until his face beamed with celestial light
That like a holy halo crowned his head.

Gently he spoke: "My dearest and my best,
The time has come — the time when we must part.
Let not your heart be troubled — it is best."
This said, a tender kiss spoke to her heart,
In love's own language, of unchanging love.
When sweet Rahula stretched his little arms,
And cooing asked his share of tenderness,
Siddartha from her bosom took their boy,
And though sore troubled, both together smiled,
And with him playing, that sweet jargon spoke,
Which, though no lexicon contains its words,
Seems like the speech of angels, poorly learned,
For every sound and syllable and word
Was filled brimful of pure and perfect love.
At length grown calm, they tenderly communed
Of all their past, of all their hopes and fears;
And when the time of separation came,
His holy resolution gave her strength
To give the last embrace and say farewell.
And forth he rode,* mounted on Kantaka,
A prince, a loving father, husband, son,
To exile driven by all-embracing love.

---

* In the "Light of Asia," the prince, after leaving his young wife, is made to pass through a somewhat extensive harem *en deshabille*, which is described with voluptuous minuteness. Although there are some things in later Buddhistic literature that seem to justify it, I can but regard the introduction of an institution so entirely alien to every age, form and degree of Aryan civilization and so inconsistent with the tender conjugal love which was the strongest tie to his beloved home, as a serious blot on that beautiful poem and as inconsistent with its whole theory, for no prophet ever came from a harem.

What wonder, as the ancient writings say,
That nature to her inmost depths was stirred,
And as he passed the birds burst forth in song,
Fearless of hawk or kite that hovered near?
What wonder that the beasts of field and wood,
And all the jungle's savage denizens,
Gathered in groups and gamboled fearlessly,
Leopards with kids and wolves with skipping lambs?
For he who rode alone, bowed down and sad,
Taught millions, crores* of millions, yet unborn
To treat with kindness every living thing.
What wonder that the deepest hells were stirred?
What wonder that the heavens were filled with joy?
For he, bowed down with sorrow, going forth,
Shall come with joy and teach all men the way
From earth's sad turmoil to Nirvana's rest.

* A crore is ten millions.

BOOK IV.

Far from his kingdom, far from home and friends,
The prince has gone, his flowing locks close shorn,
His rings and soft apparel laid aside,
All signs of rank and royalty cast off.
Clothed in a yellow robe, simple and coarse,
Through unknown streets from door to door he passed,
Holding an alms-bowl forth for willing gifts.
But when, won by his stateliness and grace,
They brought their choicest stores, he gently said:
"Not so, my friends, keep such for those who need —
The sick and old; give me but common food."
And when sufficient for the day was given,
He took a way leading without the walls,
And through rich gardens, through the fruitful fields,
Under dark mangoes and the jujube trees,
Eastward toward Sailagiri, hill of gems;
And through an ancient grove, skirting its base,
Where, soothed by every soft and tranquil sound,
Full many saints were wearing out their days
In meditation, earnest, deep, intent,

Seeking to solve the mystery of life,
Seeking, by leaving all its joys and cares,
Seeking, by doubling all its woes and pains,
To gain an entrance to eternal rest ;
And winding up its rugged sides, to where
A shoulder of the mountain, sloping west,
O'erhangs a cave with wild figs canopied.
This mountain cave was now his dwelling-place,
A stone his pillow, and the earth his bed,
His earthen alms-bowl holding all his stores
Except the crystal waters, murmuring near.
A lonely path, rugged, and rough, and steep ;
A lonely cave, its stillness only stirred
By eagle's scream, or raven's solemn croak,
Or by the distant city's softened sounds,
Save when a sudden tempest breaks above,
And rolling thunders shake the trembling hills —
A path since worn by countless pilgrims' feet,
Coming from far to view this hallowed spot,
And bow in worship on his hard, cold bed,
And press his pillow with their loving lips.
For here, for six long years, the world-renowned,
The tender lover of all living things,
Fasted and watched and wrestled for the light,
Less for himself than for a weeping world.
And here arrived, he ate his simple meal,
And then in silent meditation sat
The livelong day, heedless of noon's fierce heat
That sent to covert birds and panting beasts,
And from the parched and glowing plain sent up,
As from a furnace, gusts of scorching air,

Through which the city's walls, the rocks and
    trees.
All seemed to tremble, quiver, glow and shake,
As if a palsy shook the trembling world;
Heedless of loosened rocks that crashed so near,
And dashed and thundered to the depths below,
And of the shepherds, who with wondering awe
Came near to gaze upon his noble form
And gentle, loving but majestic face,
And thought some god had deigned to visit men.
And thus he sat, still as the rock his seat,
Seeking to pierce the void from whence man came,
To look beyond the veil that shuts him in,
To find a clue to life's dark labyrinth,
Seeking to know why man is cast adrift
Upon the bosom of a troubled sea,
His boat so frail, his helm and compass lost,
To sink at last in dull oblivion's depths;
When nature seems so perfect and complete,
Grand as a whole, and perfect all its parts,
Which from the greatest to the least proclaims
That Wisdom, Watchfulness, and Power and Love
Which built the mountains, spread the earth
    abroad,
And fixed the bounds that ocean cannot pass;
Which taught the seasons their accustomed rounds,
Lest seed-time and the happy harvests fail;
Which guides the stars in their celestial course,
And guides the pigeon's swift unerring flight
O'er mountain, sea and plain and desert waste,
Straight as an arrow to her distant home;

Teaching the ant for winter to prepare;
Clothing the lily in its princely pride;
Watching the tiny sparrow when it falls;
Nothing too great for His almighty arm;
Nothing too small for His all-seeing eye;
Nothing too mean for His paternal care.

 And thus he mused, seeking to find a light
To guide men on their dark and weary way.
And through the valley and the shades of death,
Until the glories of the setting sun
Called him to vespers and his evening meal.

 Then roused from revery, ablutions made.
Eight times he bowed, just as the setting sun,
A fiery red, sunk slowly out of sight
Beyond the western plains, gilded and tinged.
Misty and vast, beneath a brilliant sky,
Shaded from brightest gold to softest rose.
Then, after supper, back and forth he paced
Upon the narrow rock before his cave,
Seeking to ease his numbed and stiffened limbs;
While evening's sombre shadows slowly crept
From plain to hill and highest mountain-top,
And solemn silence settled on the world,
Save for the night-jar's cry and owl's complaint;
While many lights from out the city gleam,
And thickening stars spangle the azure vault,
Until the moon, with soft and silvery light,
Half veils and half reveals the sleeping world.
And then he slept — for weary souls must sleep.

As well as bodies worn with daily toil ;
And as he lay stretched on his hard, cold bed,
His youthful blood again bounds freely on,
Repairing wastes the weary day had made.
And then he dreamed. Sometimes he dreamed of home,
Of young Rahula, reaching out his arms,
Of sweet Yasodhara with loving words
Cheering him on, as love alone can cheer.
Sometimes he dreamed he saw that living light
For which his earnest soul so long had yearned —
But over hills and mountains far away.
And then he seemed with labored steps to climb
Down giddy cliffs, far harder than ascent,
While yawning chasms threatened to devour,
And beetling cliffs precluded all retreat;
But still the way seemed opening step by step,
Until he reached the valley's lowest depths,
Where twilight reigned, and grim and ghastly forms,
With flaming swords, obstruct his onward way,
But his all-conquering love still urged him on,
When with wild shrieks they vanished in thin air;
And then he climbed, clinging to jutting cliffs,
And stunted trees that from each crevice grew,
Till weary, breathless, he regained the heights,
To see that light nearer, but still so far.

    And thus he slept, and thus sometimes he dreamed,
But rose before the dawn had tinged the east,

Before the jungle-cock had made his call,
When thoughts are clearest, and the world is still,
Refreshed and strengthened for his daily search
Into the seeds of sorrow, germs of pain,
After a light to scatter doubts and fears.

But when the coming day silvered the east,
And warmed that silver into softest gold,
And faintest rose-tints tinged the passing clouds,
He, as the Vedas taught, each morning bathed
In the clear stream that murmured near his cave,
Then bowed in reverence to the rising sun,
As from behind the glittering mountain-peaks
It burst in glory on the waking world.

Then bowl and staff in hand, he took his way
Along his mountain-path and through the grove,
And through the gardens, through the fruitful fields,
Down to the city, for his daily alms;
While children his expected coming watch,
And running cry: "The gracious Rishi comes."
All gladly gave, and soon his bowl was filled,
For he repaid their gifts with gracious thanks,
And his unbounded love, clearer than words,
Spoke to their hearts as he passed gently on.
Even stolid plowmen after him would look,
Wondering that one so stately and so grand
Should even for them have kind and gracious words.
Sometimes while passing through the sacred grove,
He paused beneath an aged banyan-tree,

Whose spreading branches drooping down took
    root
To grow again in other giant trunks,
An ever-widening, ever-deepening shade,
Where five, like him in manhood's early prime,
Each bound to life by all its tender ties,
High born and rich, had left their happy homes,
Their only food chance-gathered day by day,
Their only roof this spreading banyan-tree;
And there long time they earnestly communed,
Seeking to aid each other in the search
For higher life and for a clearer light.
And here, under a sacred peepul's shade,
Two Brahmans, famed for sanctity, had dwelt
For many years, all cares of life cast off,
Who by long fastings sought to make the veil
Of flesh translucent to the inner eye;
Eyes fixed intently on the nose's tip,
To lose all consciousness of outward things;
By breath suppressed to still the outer pulse,
So that the soul might wake to conscious life,
And on unfolded wings unchecked might rise,
And in the purest auras freely soar,
Above cross-currents that engender clouds
Where thunders roll, and quick cross-lightnings
    play,
To view the world of causes and of life,
And bathe in light that knows no night, no change.
With eager questionings he sought to learn,
While they with gentle answers gladly taught
All that their self-denying search had learned.

And thus he passed his days and months and years,
In constant, patient, earnest search for light,
With longer fastings and more earnest search,
While day by day his body frailer grew,
Until his soul, loosed from its earthly bonds,
Sometimes escaped its narrow prison-house,
And like the lark to heaven's gate it soared,
To view the glories of the coming dawn.
But as he rose, the sad and sorrowing world,
For which his soul with tender love had yearned,
Seemed deeper in the nether darkness sunk,
Beyond his reach, beyond his power to save,
When sadly to his prison-house he turned,
Wishing no light that did not shine for all.

Six years had passed, six long and weary years,
Since first he left the world to seek for light.
Knowledge he found, knowledge that soared aloft
To giddy heights, and sounded hidden depths,
Secrets of knowledge that the Brahmans taught
The favored few, but far beyond the reach
Of those who toil and weep and cry for help;
A light that gilds the highest mountain-tops,
But leaves the fields and valleys dark and cold;
But not that living light for which he yearned,
To light life's humble walks and common ways,
And send its warmth to every heart and home,
As spring-time sends a warm and genial glow
To every hill and valley, grove and field,
Clothing in softest verdure common grass,
As well as sandal-trees and lofty palms.

One night, when hope seemed yielding to despair,
Sleepless he lay upon the earth — his bed —
When suddenly a white and dazzling light
Shone through the cave, and all was dark again.
Startled he rose, then prostrate in the dust,
His inmost soul breathed forth an earnest prayer *
That he who made the light would make it shine
Clearer and clearer to that perfect day,
When innocence, and peace, and righteousness
Might fill the earth, and ignorance and fear,
And cruelty and crime, might fly away,
As birds of night and savage prowling beasts
Fly from the glories of the rising sun.
Long time he lay, wrestling in earnest prayer,
When from the eastern wall, one clothed in light,
Beaming with love, and halo-crowned, appeared,
And gently said: "Siddartha, rise! go forth!
Waste not your days in fasts, your nights in tears!
Give what you have; do what you find to do;
With gentle admonitions check the strong;
With loving counsels aid and guide the weak,

---

* I am aware there are many who think that Buddha did not believe in prayer, which Arnold puts into his own mouth in these words, which sound like the clanking of chains in a prison-vault:
"Pray not! the darkness will not brighten! Ask
Nought from Silence, for it cannot speak!"
Buddha did teach that mere prayers without any effort to overcome our evils is of no more use than for a merchant to pray the farther bank of a swollen stream to come to him without seeking any means to cross, which merely differs in words from the declaration of St. James that faith without works is dead; but if he ever taught that the earnest yearning of a soul for help, which is the essence of prayer, is no aid in the struggle for a higher life, then my whole reading has been at fault, and the whole Buddhist worship has been a departure from the teachings of its founder.

And light will come, the day will surely dawn."
This said, the light grew dim, the form was gone,
But hope revived, his heart was strong again.

   Joyful he rose, and when the rising sun
Had filled the earth's dark places full of light,
With all his worldly wealth, his staff and bowl,
Obedient to that voice he left his cave;
When from a shepherd's cottage near his way,
Whence he had often heard the busy hum
Of industry, and childhood's merry laugh,
There came the angry, stern command of one
Clothed in a little brief authority,
Mingled with earnest pleadings, and the wail
Of women's voices, and above them all
The plaintive treble of a little child.
Thither he turned, and when he reached the spot,
The cause of all this sorrow was revealed:
One from the king had seized their little all,
Their goats and sheep, and e'en the child's pet lamb.
But when they saw him they had often watched
With reverent awe, as if come down from heaven,
Prostrate they fell, and kissed his garment's hem,
While he so insolent, now stood abashed,
And, self accused, he thus excused himself:
"The Brahmans make this day a sacrifice,
And they demand unblemished goats and lambs.
I but obey the king's express command
To bring them to the temple ere high noon."
But Buddha stooped and raised the little child,
Who nestled in his arms in perfect trust,

And gently said : "Rise up, my friends, weep not !
The king must be obeyed — but kings have hearts.
I go along to be your advocate.
The king may spare what zealous priest would kill,
Thinking the gods above delight in blood."
But when the officers would drive the flock
With staves and slings and loud and angry cries,
They only scattered them among the rocks,
And Buddha bade the shepherd call his own,
As love can lead where force in vain would drive.
He called ; they knew his voice and followed him,
Dumb innocents, down to the slaughter led,
While Buddha kissed the child, and followed them,
With those so late made insolent by power,
Now dumb as if led out to punishment.

    Meanwhile the temple-gates wide open stood,
And when the king, in royal purple robed,
And decked with gems, attended by his court,
To clash of cymbals, sound of shell and drum,
Through streets swept clean and sprinkled with
    perfumes,
Adorned with flags, and filled with shouting crowds,
Drew near the sacred shrine, a greater came,
Through unswept ways, where dwelt the toiling
    poor,
Huddled in wretched huts, breathing foul air,
Living in fetid filth and poverty —
No childhood's joys, youth prematurely old,
Manhood a painful struggle but to live,
And age a weary shifting of the scene ;

While all the people drew aside to gaze
Upon his gentle but majestic face,
Beaming with tender, all-embracing love.
And when the king and royal train dismount,
'Mid prostrate people and the stately priests,
On fragrant flowers that carpeted his way,
And mount the lofty steps to reach the shrine,
Siddartha came, upon the other side,
'Mid stalls for victims, sheds for sacred wood,
And rude attendants on the pompous rites,
Who seized a goat, the patriarch of the flock,
And bound him firm with sacred munja grass,
And bore aloft, while Buddha followed where
A priest before the blazing altar stood
With glittering knife, and others fed the fires,
While clouds of incense from the altar rose,
Sweeter than Araby the blest can yield,
And white-robed Brahmans chant their sacred
    hymns.
And there before that ancient shrine they met,
The king, the priests, the hermit from the hill,
When one, an aged Brahman, raised his hands,
And praying, lifted up his voice and cried:
"O hear! great Indra, from thy lofty throne
On Meru's holy mountain, high in heaven.
Let every good the king has ever done
With this sweet incense mingled rise to thee;
And every secret, every open sin
Be laid upon this goat, to sink from sight,
Drunk by the earth with his hot spouting blood,
Or on this altar with his flesh be burned."

And all the Brahman choir responsive cried:
"Long live the king! now let the victim die!"
But Buddha said: "Let him not strike, O king!
For how can God, being good, delight in blood?
And how can blood wash out the stains of sin,
And change the fixed eternal law of life
That good from good, evil from evil flows?"
This said, he stooped and loosed the panting goat,
None staying him, so great his presence was.
And then with loving tenderness he taught
How sin works out its own sure punishment;
How like corroding rust and eating moth
It wastes the very substance of the soul;
Like poisoned blood it surely, drop by drop,
Pollutes the very fountain of the life;
Like deadly drug it changes into stone
The living fibres of a loving heart;
Like fell disease, it breeds within the veins
The living agents of a living death;
And as in gardens overgrown with weeds,
Nothing but patient labor, day by day,
Uprooting cherished evils one by one,
Watering its soil with penitential tears,
Can fit the soul to grow that precious seed,
Which taking root, spreads out a grateful shade
Where gentle thoughts like singing birds may lodge,
Where pure desires like fragrant flowers may bloom,
And loving acts like ripened fruits may hang.
Then, chiding not, with earnest words he urged
Humanity to man, kindness to beasts,

Pure words, kind acts, in all our daily walks,
As better than the blood of lambs and goats,
Better than incense or the chanted hymn,
To cleanse the heart and please the powers above,
And fill the world with harmony and peace,
Till pricked in heart, the priest let fall his knife ;
The Brahmans listening, ceased to chant their
    hymns ;
The king drank in his words with eager ears ;
And from that day no altar dripped with blood,
But flowers instead breathed forth their sweet per-
    fumes.
And when that troubled day drew near its close,
Joy filled once more that shepherd's humble home.
From door to door his simple story flew,
And when the king entered his palace gates,
New thoughts were surging in his wakened soul.

  But though the beasts have lairs, the birds have
    nests,
Buddha had not whereon to lay his head,
Not even a mountain-cave to call his home ;
And forth he fared, heedless about his way —
For every way was now alike to him.
Heedless of food, his alms-bowl hung unused,
While all the people stood aside with awe,
And to their children pointed out the man
Who plead the shepherd's cause before the king.
At length he passed the city's western gate,
And crossed the little plain circling its walls,
Circled itself by five bold hills that rise,

A rugged rampart and an outer wall.
Two outer gates this mountain rampart had.
The one a narrow valley opening west
Toward Gaya, through the red Barabar hills,
Through which the rapid Phalgu swiftly glides,
Down from the Vindhya mountains far away,
Then gently winds around this fruitful plain;
Its surface green with floating lotus leaves,
And bright with lotus blossoms, blue and white,
O'erhung with drooping trees and trailing vines,
Till through the eastern gate it hastens on,
To lose itself in Gunga's sacred stream.

   Toward Gaya now Siddartha bent his steps,
Distant the journey of a single day
As men marked distance in those ancient times,
No longer heeded in this headlong age,
When we count moments by the miles we pass;
And one may see the sun sink out of sight
Behind great banks of gray and wintry clouds,
While feathery snowflakes fill the frosty air,
And after quiet sleep may wake next day
To see it bathe green fields with floods of light,
And dry the sparkling dew from opening flowers,
And hear the joyful burst of vernal song,
And breathe the balmy air of opening spring.

   And as he went, weary and faint and sad,
The valley opening showed a pleasant grove,
Where many trees mingled their grateful shade,
And many blossoms blended sweet perfumes;

And there, under a drooping vakul-tree,
A bower of roses and sweet jasmine vines,
Within a couch, without a banquet spread,
While near a fountain with its falling spray
Ruffled the surface of a shining pool,
Whose liquid cadence mingled with the songs
Of many birds concealed among the trees.

And there three seeming sister graces were,*
Fair as young Venus rising from the sea.
The one in seeming childlike innocence
Bathed in the pool, while her low liquid laugh
Rung sweet and clear; and one her vina tuned,
And as she played, the other lightly danced,
Clapping her hands, tinkling her silver bells,
Whose gauzy silken garments seemed to show
Rather than hide her slender, graceful limbs.
And she who played the vina sweetly sang:

> "Come to our bower and take your rest—
> Life is a weary road at best.
> Eat, for your board is richly spread;
> Drink, for your wine is sparkling red:
> Rest, for the weary day is past;
> Sleep, for the shadows gather fast.
> Tune not your vina-strings too high.
> Strained they will break and the music die.
> Come to our bower and take your rest —
> Life is a weary road at best."

* Mara dispatched three pleasure-girls from the north quarter to come and tempt him. Their names were Tanha, Rati and Ranga. Fa Hian (Beal), p. 120.

But Buddha, full of pity, passing said :
" Alas, poor soul ! flitting a little while
Like painted butterflies before the lamp
That soon will burn your wings ; like silly doves,
Calling the cruel kite to seize and kill ;
Displaying lights to be the robber's guide ;
Enticing men to wrong, who soon despise.
Ah ! poor, perverted, cold and cruel world !
Delights of love become the lures of lust,
The joys of heaven changed into fires of hell."

BOOK V.

Now mighty Mara, spirit of the air,
The prince of darkness, ruling worlds below,
Had watched for Buddha all these weary years,
Seeking to lead his steady steps astray
By many wiles his wicked wit devised,
Lest he at length should find the living light
And rescue millions from his dark domains.
Now, showing him the kingdoms of the world,
He offered him the Chakravartin's crown;
Now, opening seas of knowledge, shoreless, vast,
Knowledge of ages past and yet to come,
Knowledge of nature and the hidden laws
That guide her changes, guide the rolling spheres,
Sakwal on sakwal,* boundless, infinite,
Yet ever moving on in harmony,
He thought to puff his spirit up with pride
Till he should quite forget a suffering world,
In sin and sorrow groping blindly on.

---

*A sakwal was a sun with its system of worlds, which the ancient Hindoos believed extended one beyond another through infinite space. It indicates great advance in astronomical knowledge when such a complex idea, now universally received as true, as that the fixed stars are suns with systems of worlds like ours, could be expressed in a single word.

But when he saw that lust of power moved not,
And thirst for knowledge turned him not aside
From earnest search after the living light,
From tender love for every living thing,
He sent the tempters Doubt and dark Despair.
And as he watched for final victory
He saw that light flash through the silent cave,
And heard the Buddha breathe that earnest prayer,
And fled amazed, nor dared to look behind.
For though to Buddha all his way seemed dark,
His wily enemy could see a Power,
A mighty Power, that ever hovered near,
A present help in every time of need,
When sinking souls seek earnestly for aid.
He fled, indeed, as flies the prowling wolf,
Alarmed at watch-dog's bark or shepherd's voice,
While seeking entrance to the slumbering fold,
But soon returns with soft and stealthy step,
With keenest scent snuffing the passing breeze,
With ears erect catching each slightest sound,
With glaring eyes watching each moving thing,
With hungry jaws, skulking about the fold
Till coming dawn drives him to seek his lair.
So Mara fled, and so he soon returned,
And thus he watched the Buddha's every step ;
Saw him with gentleness quell haughty power ;
Saw him with tenderness raise up the weak ;
Heard him before the Brahmans and the king
Denounce those bloody rites ordained by him ;
Heard him declare the deadly work of Sin,
His own prime minister and eldest-born ;

Heard him proclaim the mighty power of Love
To cleanse the life and make the flinty heart
As soft as sinews of the new-born babe.
And when he saw whither he bent his steps,
He sent three wrinkled hags, deformed and foul,
The willing agents of his wicked will —
Life-wasting Idleness, the thief of time;
Lascivious Lust, whose very touch defiles,
Poisoning the blood, polluting all within;
And greedy Gluttony, most gross of all,
Whose ravening maw forever asks for more —
To that delightful garden near his way,
To tempt the Master, their true forms concealed —
For who so gross that such coarse hags could tempt? —
But clothed instead in youthful beauty's grace.
And now he saw him pass unmoved by lust,
Nor yet with cold, self-righteous pride puffed up,
But breathing pity from his inmost soul
E'en for the ministers of vice themselves.

  Defeated, not discouraged, still he thought
To try one last device, for well he knew
That Buddha's steps approached the sacred tree
Where light would dawn and all his power would end.
Upon a seat beside the shaded path,
A seeming aged Brahman, Mara sat,
And when the prince approached, his tempter rose,
Saluting him with gentle stateliness,
Saluted in return with equal grace.

"Whither away, my son?" the tempter said,
"If you to Gaya now direct your steps,
Perhaps your youth may cheer my lonely age."
"I go to seek for light," the prince replied,
"But where it matters not, so light be found."

But Mara answered him: "Your search is vain.
Why seek to know more than the Vedas teach?
Why seek to learn more than the teachers know?
But such is youth; the rosy tints of dawn
Tinge all his thoughts. 'Excelsior!' he cries,
And fain would scale the unsubstantial clouds
To find a light that knows no night, no change;
We Brahmans chant our hymns in solemn wise,
The vulgar listen with profoundest awe;
But still our muffled heart-throbs beat the march
Onward, forever onward, to the grave,
When one ahead cries, 'Lo! I see a light!'
And others clutch his garments, following on
Till all in starless darkness disappear.
There may be day beyond this starless night,
There may be life beyond this dark profound —
But who has ever seen that changeless day?
What steps have e'er retraced that silent road?
Fables there are, hallowed by hoary age,
Fables and ancient creeds, that men have made
To give them power with ignorance and fear;
Fables of gods with human passions filled;
Fables of men who walked and talked with gods;
Fables of kalpas passed, when Brahma slept
And all created things were wrapped in flames,

And then the floods descended, chaos reigned,
The world a waste of waters, and the heavens
A sunless void, until again he wakes,
And sun and moon and stars resume their rounds,
Oceans receding show the mountain-tops,
And then the hills and spreading plains —
Strange fables all, that crafty men have feigned.
Why waste your time pursuing such vain dreams —
As some benighted travelers chase false lights
To lose themselves in bogs and fens at last?
But read instead in Nature's open book
How light from darkness grew by slow degrees;
How crawling worms grew into light-winged birds,
Acquiring sweetest notes and gayest plumes;
How lowly ferns grew into lofty palms;
How men have made themselves from chattering
    apes;*
How, even from protoplasm to highest bard,
Selecting and rejecting, mind has grown
Until at length all secrets are unlocked,
And man himself now stands pre-eminent,
Maker and master of his own great self,
To sneer at all his lisping childlike past
And laugh at all his fathers had revered."

    The prince with gentle earnestness replied:
"Full well I know how blindly we grope on

    *It may seem like an anachronism to put the very words of the modern agnostic into the mouth of Buddha's tempter, but these men are merely threshing over old straw. The sneer of Epicurus curled the lip of Voltaire, and now merely breaks out into a broad laugh on the good-natured face of Ingersoll.

In doubt and fear and ignorance profound,
The wisdom of the past a book now sealed.
But why despise what ages have revered?
As some rude plowman casts on rubbish-heaps
The rusty casket that his share reveals,
Not knowing that within it are concealed
Most precious gems, to make him rich indeed,
The hand that hid them from the robber, cold,
The key that locked this rusty casket, lost.
The past was wise, else whence that wondrous tongue*
That we call sacred, which the learned speak,
Now passing out of use as too refined
For this rude age, too smooth for our rough tongues,
Too rich and delicate for our coarse thoughts.
Why should such men make fables so absurd
Unless within their rough outside is stored
Some precious truth from profanation hid?
Revere your own, revile no other faith,
Lest with the casket you reject the gems,
Or with rough hulls reject the living seed.
Doubtless in nature changes have been wrought
That speak of ages in the distant past,
Whose contemplation fills the mind with awe.
The smooth-worn pebbles on the highest hills
Speak of an ocean sweeping o'er their tops;
The giant palms, now changed to solid rocks,

---

*The Sanscrit, the most perfect of all languages, and the mother of Greek and of all the languages of the Aryan races, now spread over the world, had gone out of use in Buddha's time, and the Pali, one of its earliest offspring, was used by the great teacher and his people.

Speak of the wonders of a buried world.
Why seek to solve the riddle nature puts,
Of whence and why, with theories and dreams?
The crawling worm proclaims its Maker's power;
The singing bird proclaims its Maker's skill;
The mind of man proclaims a greater Mind,
Whose will makes world, whose thoughts are living acts.
Our every heart-throb speaks of present power,
Preserving, recreating, day by day.
Better confess how little we can know,
Better with feet unshod and humble awe
Approach this living Power to ask for aid."
And as he spoke the devas filled the air,
Unseen, unheard of men, and sweetly sung:
"Hail, prince of peace! hail, harbinger of day!
The darkness vanishes, the light appears."
But Mara heard, and silent slunk away.
The o'erwrought prince fell prostrate on the ground
And lay entranced, while devas hovered near,
Watching each heart-throb, breathing that sweet calm
Its guardian angel gives the sleeping child.

The night has passed, the day-star fades from sight,
And morning's softest tint of rose and gold
Tinges the east and tips the mountain-tops.
The silent village stirs with waking life,
The bleat of goats and low of distant herds,

The song of birds and crow of jungle-cocks
Breathe softest music through the dewy air.

And now two girls,* just grown to womanhood,
The lovely daughters of the village lord,
Trapusha one, and one Balika called,
Up with the dawn, trip lightly o'er the grass,
Bringing rich curds and rice picked grain by grain,
A willing offering to their guardian god —
Who dwelt, as all the simple folk believed,
Beneath an aged bodhi-tree that stood
Beside the path and near where Buddha lay —
To ask such husbands as their fancies paint,
Gentle and strong, and noble, true and brave;
And having left their gifts and made their vows,
With timid steps the maidens stole away.

But while the outer world is filled with life,
That inner world from whence this life proceeds,
Concealed from sight by matter's blinding folds,
Whose coarser currents fill with wondrous power
The nervous fluid of the universe
Which darts through nature's frame, from star to star,
From cloud to cloud, filling the world with awe;
Now harnessed to our use, a patient drudge,
Heedless of time or space, bears human thought

---

* Arnold follows the tradition that there was but one, whom he makes a young wife, without any authority so far as I can learn. I prefer to follow the Chinese pilgrim, Fa Hian, who was on the ground with every means of knowing, who makes them two young girls, and named as above.

From land to land and through the ocean's depths;
And bears the softest tones of human speech
Faster than light, farther than ocean sounds;
And whirls the clattering car through crowded streets,
And floods with light the haunts of prowling thieves —
That inner world, whose very life is love,
Pure love, and perfect, infinite, intense,
That world is now astir. A rift appears
In those dark clouds that rise from sinful souls
And hide from us its clear celestial light,
And clouds of messengers from that bright world,
Whom they called devas and we angels call,
Rush to that rift to rescue and to save.
The wind from their bright wings fanned Buddha's soul,
The love from their sweet spirits warmed his heart.
He starts from sleep, but rising, scarcely knows
If he had seen a vision while awake,
Or, sunk in sleep, had dreamed a heavenly dream.
From that pure presence all his tempters fled.
The calm of conflict ended filled his soul,
And led by unseen hands he forward passed
To where the sacred fig-tree long had grown,
Beneath whose shade the village altar stood,
Where simple folk would place their willing gifts,
And ask the aid their simple wants required,
Believing all the life above, around,
The life within themselves, must surely come
From living powers that ever hovered near.

Here lay the food Sagata's daughters brought,
The choicest products of his herds and fields.
This grateful food met nature's every need,
Diffused a healthful glow through all his frame,
And all the body's eager yearnings stilled.
Seven days he sat, and ate no more nor drank,
Yet hungered not, nor burned with parching thirst,
For heavenly manna fed his hungry soul —
Its wants were satisfied, the body's ceased.
Seven days he sat, in sweet internal peace
Waiting for light, and sure that light would come,
When seeming scales fell from his inner sight,
His spirit's eyes were opened and he saw
Not far away, but near, within, above,
As dwells the soul within this mortal frame,
A world within this workday world of ours,
The living soul of all material things.

   Eastward he saw a never-setting Sun,
Whose light is truth, the light of all the worlds,
Whose heat is tender, all-embracing love,
The inmost Life of everything that lives,
The mighty Prototype and primal Cause
Of all the suns that light this universe,
From ours, full-orbed, that tints the glowing east
And paints the west a thousand varied shades,
To that far distant little twinkling star
That seems no larger than the glow-worm's lamp,
Itself a sun to light such worlds as ours;
And round about Him clouds of living light,
Bright clouds of cherubim and seraphim,

Who sing His praise and execute His will —
Not idly singing, as the foolish feign,
But voicing forth their joy they work and sing;
Doing His will, their works sound forth His praise.

On every side were fields of living green,
With gardens, groves and gently rising hills,
Where crystal streams of living waters flow,
And dim with distance Meru's lofty heights.
No desert sands, no mountains crowned with ice,
For here the scorching simoom never blows,
Nor wintry winds, that pierce and freeze and kill,
But gentle breezes breathing sweet perfumes;
No weeds, no thorns, no bitter poisonous fruits,
No noxious reptiles and no prowling beasts;
For in this world of innocence and love
No evil thoughts give birth to evil things,
But many birds of every varied plume
Delight the ear with sweetest melody;
And many flowers of every varied tint
Fill all the air with odors rich and sweet;
And many fruits, suited to every taste,
Hang ripe and ready that who will may eat —
A world of life, with all its lights and shades,
The bright original of our sad world
Without its sin and storms, its thorns and tears.
No Lethe's sluggish waters lave its shores,
Nor solemn shades, of poet's fancy bred,
Sit idly here to boast of battles past,
Nor wailing ghosts wring here their shadowy hands
For lack of honor to their cast-off dust;

But living men, in human bodies clothed —
Not bodies made of matter, dull and coarse,
Dust from the dust and soon to dust returned,
But living bodies, clothing living souls,
Bodies responsive to the spirit's will,
Clothing in acts the spirit's inmost thoughts —
Dwell here in many mansions, large and fair,
Stretching beyond the keenest vision's ken,
With room for each and more than room for all,
Forever filling and yet never full.
Not clogged by matter, fast as fleetest birds,
Wishing to go, they go; to come, they come.
No helpless infancy or palsied age,
But all in early manhood's youthful bloom,
The old grown young, the child to man's estate.
Gentle they seemed as they passed to and fro,
Gentle and strong, with every manly grace;
Busy as bees in summer's sunny hours,
In works of usefulness and acts of love;
No pinching poverty or grasping greed,
Gladly receiving, they more gladly give,
Sharing in peace the bounties free to all.

As lost in wonder and delight he gazed,
He saw approaching from a pleasant grove
Two noble youths, yet full of gentleness,
Attending one from sole to crown a queen,
With every charm of fresh and blooming youth
And every grace of early womanhood,
Her face the mirror of her gentle soul,
Her flowing robes finer than softest silk,

That as she moved seemed woven of the light ;
Not borne by clumsy wings, or labored steps,
She glided on as if her will had wings
That bore her willing body where she wished.
As she approached, close by her side he saw,
As through a veil or thin transparent mist,
The form and features of the aged king,
Older and frailer by six troubled years
Than when they parted, yet his very face,
Whom she was watching with the tenderest care.
And nearer seen each seeming youth was two,
As when at first in Eden's happy shade
Our primal parents ere the tempter came
Were twain, and yet but one, so on they come,
Hand joined in hand, heart beating close to heart,
One will their guide and sharing every thought,
Beaming with tender, all-embracing love,
Whom God had joined and death had failed to part.

    What need of words to introduce his guests ?
Love knows her own, the mother greets her son.
Her parents and the king's, who long had watched
Their common offspring with a constant care,
Inspiring hope and breathing inward peace
When secret foes assailed on every side,
Now saw him burst the clouds that veiled their view
And stand triumphant full before their eyes.
O happy meeting ! joy profound, complete !
Soul greeting soul, heart speaking straight to heart,
While countless happy faces hovered near
And songs of joy sound through Nirvana's heights.

At length, the transports of first meeting past,
More of this new-found world he wished to see,
More of its peace and joy he wished to know.
Led by his loving guides, enwrapt he saw
Such scenes of beauty passing human speech,
Such scenes of peace and joy past human thought,
That he who sings must tune a heavenly lyre
And seraphs touch his lips with living fire.
My unanointed lips will not presume
To try such lofty themes, glad if I gain
A distant prospect of the promised land,
And catch some glimpses through the gates ajar.
Long time he wandered through these blissful scenes,
Time measured by succession of delights,
Till wearied by excess of very joy
Both soul and body sunk in tranquil sleep.
He slept while hosts of devas sweetly sung:
"Hail, great physician! savior, lover, friend!
Joy of the worlds, guide to Nirvana, hail!"
From whose bright presence Mara's myriads fled.
But Mara's self, subtlest of all, fled not,
But putting on a seeming yogi's form,
Wasted, as if by fasts, to skin and bone,
On one foot standing, rooted to the ground,
The other raised against his fleshless thigh,
Hands stretched aloft till joints had lost their use,
And clinched so close, as if in firm resolve,
The nails had grown quite through the festering palms,*

*Bishop Heber says he saw a recluse whose hands had been clinched so close and so long that the nails had actually grown through the hands as here described.

His tattered robes, as if worn out by age,
Hanging like moss from trees decayed and dead,
While birds were nesting in his tangled hair.
And thus disguised the subtle Mara stood.
And when the master roused him from his sleep
His tempter cried in seeming ecstasy:
"O! happy wakening! joy succeeding grief!
Peace after trouble! rest that knows no end!
Life after death! Nirvana found at last!
Here let us wait till wasted by decay
The body's worn-out fetters drop away."

"Much suffering brother," Buddha answered him,
"The weary traveler, wandering through the night
In doubt and darkness, gladly sees the dawn.
The storm-tossed sailor on the troubled sea,
Wearied and drenched, with joy re-enters port.
But other nights succeed that happy dawn,
And other seas may toss that sailor's bark.
But he who sees Nirvana's sacred Sun,
And in Nirvana's haven furls his sails,
No more shall wander through the starless night,
No more shall battle with the winds and waves.
O joy of joys! our eyes have seen that Sun!
Our sails have almost reached that sheltering port.
But shall we, joyful at our own escape,
Leave our poor brothers battling with the storm,
Sails rent, barks leaking, helm and compass lost,
No light to guide, no hope to cheer them on?"

"Each for himself must seek, as we have sought,"

The tempter said, "and each must climb alone
The rugged path our weary feet have trod.
No royal road leads to Nirvana's rest;
No royal captain guides his army there.
Why leave the heights with so much labor gained?
Why plunge in darkness we have just escaped?
Men will not heed the message we may bring.
The great will scorn, the rabble will deride,*
And cry 'He hath a devil and is mad.'"

 "True," answered Buddha, "each must seek to find;
Each for himself must leave the downward road;
Each for himself must choose the narrow path
That leads to purity and peace and life.
But helping hands will aid those struggling up;
A warning voice may check those hasting down.
Men are like lilies in yon shining pool:
Some sunk in evil grovel in the dust,
Loving like swine to wallow in the mire —
Like those that grow within its silent depths,
Scarce raised above its black and oozy bed;
While some love good, and seek the purest light,
Breathing sweet fragrance from their gentle lives —
Like those that rise above its glassy face,
Sparkling with dewdrops, royally arrayed,
Drinking the brightness of the morning sun,
Distilling odors through the balmy air;
But countless multitudes grope blindly on,

---

*The last temptation of Buddha was to keep his light to himself under the fear that men would reject his message.

Shut out from light and crushed by cruel castes,
Willing to learn, whom none will deign to teach,
Willing to rise, whom none will deign to guide,
Who from the cradle to the silent grave,
Helpless and hopeless, only toil and weep —
Like those that on the stagnant waters float,
Smothered with leaves, covered with ropy slime,
That from the rosy dawn to dewy eve
Scarce catch one glimmer of the glorious sun.
The good scarce need, the bad will scorn, my aid ;
But these poor souls will gladly welcome help.
Welcome to me the scorn of rich and great,
Welcome the Brahman's proud and cold disdain,
Welcome revilings from the rabble rout.
If I can lead some groping souls to light —
If I can give some weary spirits rest.
Farewell, my brother, you have earned release —
Rest here in peace. I go to aid the poor."
And as he spoke a flash of lurid light
Shot through the air, and Buddha stood alone —
Alone ! to teach the warring nations peace !
Alone ! to lead a groping world to light !
Alone ! to give the heavy-laden rest !

BOOK VI.

Seven days had passed since first he saw the light,
Seven days of deep, ecstatic peace and joy,
Of open vision of that blissful world,
Of sweet communion with those dwelling there.
But having tasted, seen and felt the joys
Of that bright world where love is all in all,
Filling each heart, inspiring every thought,
Guiding each will and prompting every act,
He yearned to see the other, darker side
Of that bright picture, where the wars and hates,
The lust, the greed, the cruelty and crime
That fill the world with pain and want and woe
Have found their dwelling-place and final goal.

Quicker than eagles soaring toward the sun
Till but a speck against the azure vault
Swoop down upon their unsuspecting prey,
Quicker than watch-fires on the mountain-top
Send warnings to the dwellers in the plain,
Led by his guides he reached Nirvana's verge,
Whence he beheld a broad and pleasant plain,
Spread with a carpet of the richest green
And decked with flowers of every varied tint,

Whose blended odors fill the balmy air,
Where trees, pleasant to sight and good for food,
In rich abundance and spontaneous grow.
A living stream, as purest crystal clear,
With gentle murmurs wound along the plain,
Its surface bright with fairer lotus-flowers
Than mortal eye on earth had ever seen,
While on its banks were cool, umbrageous groves
Whose drooping branches spicy breezes stir,
A singing bird in every waving bough,
Whose joyful notes the soul of music shed.

   A mighty multitude, beyond the power
Of men to number, moved about the plain;
Some, seeming strangers, wander through the
    groves
And pluck the flowers or eat the luscious fruits;
Some, seeming visitors from better worlds,
Here wait and watch as for expected guests;
While angel devas, clothed in innocence,
Whose faces beam with wisdom, glow with love,
With loving welcomes greet each coming guest,
With loving counsels aid, instruct and guide.
And as he looked, the countless, restless throng
Seemed ever changing, ever moving on,
So that this plain, comparing great to small,
Seemed like a station near some royal town,
Greater than London or old Babylon,
Where all the roads from some vast empire meet,
And many caravans or sweeping trains
Bring and remove the ever-changing throng.

This plain a valley bordered, deep and still,
The very valley of his fearful dream
Seen from the other side, whose rising mists
Were all aglow with ever-changing light,
Like passing clouds above the setting sun,
Through which as through a glass he darkly saw
Unnumbered funeral-trains, in sable clad,
To solemn music and with measured tread
Bearing their dead to countless funeral-piles,
As thick as heaps that through the livelong day
With patient toil the sturdy woodmen rear,
While clearing forests for the golden grain,
And set aflame when evening's shades descend,
Filling the glowing woods with floods of light
And ghostly shadows: So these funeral-piles
Send up their curling smoke and crackling flames.

There eager flames devour an infant's flesh;
Here loving arms that risen infant clasp;
There loud laments bewail a loved one lost;
Here joyful welcomes greet that loved one found.
And there he saw a pompous funeral-train,
Bearing a body clothed in robes of state,
To blare of trumpet, sound of shell and drum,
While many mourners bow in silent grief,
And widows, orphans raise a loud lament
As for a father, a protector lost;
And as the flames lick up the fragrant oils,
And whirl and hiss around that wasting form,
An eager watcher from a better world
Welcomes her husband to her open arms,

The cumbrous load of pomp and power cast off,
While waiting devas and the happy throng
His power protected and his bounty blessed
With joy conduct his unaccustomed steps
Onward and upward, to those blissful seats
Where all his stores of duties well performed,
Of power well used and wealth in kindness given,
Were garnered up beyond the reach of thieves,
Where moths ne'er eat and rust can ne'er corrupt.

Another train draws near a funeral-pile,
Of aloes, sandal-wood and cassia built,
And drenched with every incense-breathing oil,
And draped with silks and rich with rarest flowers,
Where grim officials clothed in robes of state
Placed one in royal purple, decked with gems,
Whose word had been a trembling nation's law.
Whose angry nod was death to high or low.
No mourners gather round this costly pile;
The people shrink in terror from the sight.
But sullen soldiers there keep watch and ward
While eager flames consume those nerveless hands
So often raised to threaten or command,
Suck out those eyes that filled the court with fear,
And only left of all this royal pomp
A little dust the winds may blow away.

But here that selfsame monarch comes in view,
For royal purple clothed in filthy rags,
And lusterless that crown of priceless gems;
Those eyes, whose bend so lately awed the world,

Blinking and bleared and blinded by the light;
Those hands, that late a royal scepter bore,
Shaking with fear and dripping all with blood.
And as he looked that some should give him place
And lead him to a seat for monarchs fit,
He only saw a group of innocents
His hands had slain, now clothed in spotless white,
From whom he fled as if by furies chased,
Fled from those groves and gardens of delight,
Fled on and down a broad and beaten road
By many trod, and toward a desert waste
With distance dim, and gloomy, grim and vast,
Where piercing thorns and leafless briars grow,
And dead sea-apples, ashes to the taste,
Where loathsome reptiles crawl and hiss and sting,
And birds of night and bat-winged dragons fly,
Where beetling cliffs seem threatening instant fall,
And opening chasms seem yawning to devour,
And sulphurous seas were swept with lurid flames
That seethe and boil from hidden fires below.

 Again he saw, beyond that silent vale,
One frail and old, without a rich man's gate
Laid down to die beneath a peepul-tree,
And parched with thirst and pierced with sudden
  pain,
A root his pillow and the earth his bed;
Alone he met the King of terrors there;
Whose wasting body, cumbering now the ground,
Chandalas cast upon the passing stream
To float and fester in the fiery sun,

Till whirled by eddies, caught by roots, it lay
A prey for vultures and for fishes food.

  That selfsame day a dart of deadly pain
Shot through that rich man's hard, unfeeling
    heart,
That laid him low, beyond the power to save,
E'en while his servants cast without his gates
That poor old man, who came to beg him spare
His roof-tree, where his fathers all had died,
His hearth, the shrine of all his inmost joys,
His little home, to every heart so dear;
And in due season tongues of hissing flames
That rich man's robes like snowflakes whirled in
    air,
And curled his crackling skin, consumed his flesh,
And sucked the marrow from his whitened bones.

  But here these two their places seem to change.
That rich man's houses, lands, and flocks and herds,
His servants, rich apparel, stores of gold,
And all he loved and lived for left behind,
The friends that nature gave him turned to foes,
Dependents whom his greed had wronged and
    crushed
Shrinking away as from a deadly foe;
No generous wish, no gentle, tender thought
To hide his nakedness, his shriveled soul
Stood stark and bare, the gaze of passers-by;
Nothing within to draw him on and up,
He slinks away, and wanders on and down,

Till in the desert, groveling in the dust,
He digs and burrows, seeking treasures there —
While that poor man, as we count poverty,
Is rich in all that makes the spirit's wealth,
His heart so pure that thoughts of guile
And evil purpose find no lodgment there;
His life so innocent that bitter words
And evil-speaking ne'er escape his lips;
The little that he had he freely shared,
And wished it more that more he might have given;
Now rich in soul — for here a crust of bread
In kindness shared, a cup of water given,
Is worth far more than all Potosi's mines,
And Araby's perfumes and India's silks,
And all the cattle on a thousand hills —
And clothed as with a robe of innocence
The devas welcome him, his troubles passed,
The conflict ended and the triumph gained.

And there two Brahmans press their funeral-pile,
And sink to dust amid the whirling flames.
Each from his lisping infancy had heard
That Brahmans were a high and holy caste,
Too high and holy for the common touch,
And each had learned the Vedas' sacred lore.
But here they parted. One was cold and proud,
Drawing away from all the humbler castes
As made to toil, and only fit to serve.
The other found within those sacred books
That all were brothers, made of common clay,
And filled with life from one eternal source,

While Brahmans only elder brothers were,
With greater light to be his brother's guide,
With greater strength to give his brother aid;
That he alone a real Brahman was
Who had a Brahman's spirit, not his blood.
With patient toil from youth to hoary age
He taught the ignorant and helped the weak.
And now they come where all external pomp
And rank and caste and creed are nothing worth.
But when that proud and haughty Brahman saw
Poor Sudras and Chandalas clothed in white,
He swept away with proud and haughty scorn,
Swept on and down where heartless selfishness
Alone can find congenial company.
The other, full of joy, his brothers met,
And in sweet harmony they journeyed on
Where higher joys await the pure in heart.

   And there he saw all ranks and grades and castes,
Chandala, Sudra, warrior, Brahman, prince,
The wise and ignorant, the strong and weak,
In all the stages of our mortal round
From lisping infancy to palsied age,
By all the ways to human frailty known,
Enter that vale of shadows, deep and still,
Leaving behind their pomp and power and wealth.
Leaving their rags and wretchedness and want,
And cast-off bodies, dust to dust returned,
By flames consumed or moldering to decay,
While here the real character appeared,
All shows, hypocrisies and shams cast off,

So that a life of gentleness and love
Shines through the face and molds the outer form
To living beauty, blooming not to fade,
While every act of cruelty and crime
Seems like a gangrened ever-widening wound,
Wasting the very substance of the soul,
Marring its beauty, eating out its strength.

   And here arrived, the good, in little groups
Together drawn by inward sympathy,
And led by devas, take the upward way
To those sweet fields his opened eyes had seen,
Those ever-widening mansions of delight;
While those poor souls — O sad and fearful sight! —
The very well-springs of the life corrupt,
Shrink from the light and shun the pure and good,
Fly from the devas, who with perfect love
Would gladly soothe their anguish, ease their pain,
Fly on and down that broad and beaten road,
Till in the distance in the darkness lost.
Lost! lost! and must it be forever lost?
The gentle Buddha's all-embracing love
Shrunk from the thought, but rather sought relief
In that most ancient faith by sages taught,
That these poor souls at length may find escape,
The grasping in the gross and greedy swine,
The cunning in the sly and prowling fox,
The cruel in some ravening beast of prey;
While those less hardened, less depraved, may gain

Rebirth in men, degraded, groveling, base.*
  But here in sadness let us drop the veil,
Hoping that He whose ways are not like ours,
Whose love embraces all His handiwork,
Who in beginnings sees the final end,
May find some way to save these sinful souls
Consistent with His fixed eternal law
That good from good, evil from evil flows.

  Here Buddha saw the mystery of life
At last unfolded to its hidden depths.
He saw that selfishness was sorrow's root,
And ignorance its dense and deadly shade;
He saw that selfishness bred lust and hate,
Deformed the features, and defiled the soul
And closed its windows to those waves of love
That flow perennial from Nirvana's Sun.
He saw that groveling lusts and base desires
Like noxious weeds unchecked luxurious grow,
Making a tangled jungle of the soul,
Where no good seed can find a place to root,
Where noble purposes and pure desires
And gentle thoughts wither and fade and die
Like flowers beneath the deadly upas-tree.
He saw that selfishness bred grasping greed,
And made the miser, made the prowling thief,
And bred hypocrisy, pretense, deceit,

---

* The later Buddhists make much of the doctrine of metempsychosis, but in the undoubted sayings and Sutras or sermons of Buddha I find no mention of it except in this way as the last hope of those who persist through life in evil, while the good after death reach the other shore, or Nirvana, where there is no more birth or death.

And made the bigot, made the faithless priest,
Bred anger, cruelty, and thirst for blood,
And made the tyrant, stained the murderer's knife,
And filled the world with war and want and woe,
And filled the dismal regions of the lost
With fiery flames of passions never quenched,
With sounds of discord, sounds of clanking chains,
With cries of anguish, howls of bitter hate,
Yet saw that man was free — not bound and chained*
Helpless and hopeless to a whirling wheel,
Rolled on resistless by some cruel power,
Regardless of their cries and prayers and tears —
Free to resist those gross and groveling lusts,
Free to obey Nirvana's law of love,
The law of order — primal, highest law —
Which guides the great Artificer himself,
Who weaves the garments of the joyful spring,
Who paints the glories of the passing clouds,
Who tunes the music of the rolling spheres,
Guided by love in all His mighty works,
Filling with love the humblest willing heart.

He saw that love softens and sweetens life,
And stills the passions, soothes the troubled breast,
Fills homes with joy and gives the nations peace,

---

*This great and fundamental truth, lying as the basis of human action and responsibility, was recognized by Homer, who makes Jupiter say:

"Perverse mankind, whose wills created free,
Charge all their woes to absolute decree."
Odyssey, Book I, lines 41 and 42

A sovereign balm for all the spirit's wounds,
The living fountain of Nirvana's bliss;
For here before his eyes were countless souls,
Born to the sorrows of a sinful world,
With burdens bowed, by cares and griefs oppressed,
Who felt for others' sorrows as their own,
Who lent a helping hand to those in need,
Returning good for evil, love for hate,
Whose garments now were white as spotless wool,
Whose faces beamed with gentleness and love,
As onward, upward, devas guide their steps,
Nirvana's happy mansions full in view.

   He saw the noble eightfold path that mounts
From life's low levels to Nirvana's heights.
Not by steep grades the strong alone can climb,
But by such steps as feeblest limbs may take.
He saw that day by day and step by step,
By lusts resisted and by evil shunned,
By acts of love and daily duties done,
Soothing some heartache, helping those in need,
Smoothing life's journey for a brother's feet,
Guarding the lips from harsh and bitter words,
Guarding the heart from gross and selfish thoughts,
Guarding the hands from every evil act,
Brahman or Sudra, high or low, may rise
Till heaven's bright mansions open to the view,
And heaven's warm sunshine brightens all the way;
While neither hecatombs of victims slain,
Nor clouds of incense wafted to the skies,

Nor chanted hymns, nor prayers to all the gods,
Can raise a soul that clings to groveling lusts.

   He saw the cause of sorrow, and its cure.
He saw that waves of love surround the soul
As waves of sunlight fill the outer world,
While selfishness, the subtle alchemist
Concealed within, changes that love to hate,
Forges the links of karma's fatal chain,
Of passions, envies, lusts to bind the soul,
And weaves his webs of falsehood and deceit
To close its windows to the living light,
Changing its mansion to its prison-house,
Where it must lay self-chained and self-condemned;
While DHARMA, TRUTH, the LAW, the LIVING WORD,
Brushes away those deftly woven webs,
Opens its windows to the living light,
Reveals the architect of all its ills,
Scatters the timbers of its prison-house,*
And snaps in twain those bitter, galling chains
So that the soul once more may stand erect,
Victor of self, no more to be enslaved,
And live in charity and gentle peace,
Bearing all meekly, loving those who hate;
And when at last the fated stream is reached,

---

  * After examining the attempted explanations of that remarkable passage, the original of which is given at the end of the sixth book of Arnold's "Light of Asia," I am satisfied this is its true interpretation. It is not the death of the body, for he lived forty-five years afterwards, much less the annihilation of the soul, as some have imagined, but the conquest of the passions and gross and selfish desires which make human life a prison, the very object and end of the highest Christian teachings and aspirations.

With lightened boat to reach the other shore.
And here he found the light he long had sought,
Gilding at once Nirvana's blissful heights
And lighting life's sequestered, lowly vales—
A light whose inner life is perfect love,
A love whose outer form is living light,
Nirvana's Sun, the Light of all the worlds,*
Heart of the universe, whose mighty pulse
Gives heaven, the worlds and even hell their life,
Maker and Father of all living things
Matreya's † self, the Lover, Saviour, Guide,
The last, the greatest Buddha, who must rule
As Lord of all before the kalpa's end.

The way of life—the noble eightfold path,
The way of truth, the Dharma-pada—found,
With joy he bade his loving guides farewell,
With joy he turned from all those blissful scenes.
And when the rosy dawn next tinged the east,
And morning's burst of song had waked the day,

---

* " Know then that heaven and earth's compacted frame,
And flowing waters, and the starry flame,
And both the radiant lights, one common soul
Inspires and feeds and animates the whole."
                        Dryden's Virgil, Book VI, line 360.

† Buddha predicted that Matreya (Love incarnate) would be his successor (see Beal's Fa Hian, page 137, note 2, and page 162; also Hardy's Manual, page 386, and Oldenburgh's Buddhism, page 386), who was to come at the end of five hundred years at the end of his Dharma (see Buddhism and Christianity, Lillie, page 2).

It is a remarkable fact that this successor is the most common object of worship among Buddhists, so that the most advanced Buddhists and the most earnest Christians have the same object of worship under different names.

With staff and bowl he left the sacred tree —
Where pilgrims, passing pathless mountain-heights,
And desert sands, and ocean's stormy waves,
From every nation, speaking every tongue,
Should come in after-times to breathe their vows —
Beginning on that day his pilgrimage
Of five and forty years from place to place,
Breaking the cruel chains of caste and creed,
Teaching the law of love, the way of life.

BOOK VII.

Alone on his great mission going forth,
Down Phalgu's valley he retraced his steps,
Down past the seat where subtle Mara sat,
And past the fountain where the siren sang,
And past the city, through the fruitful fields
And gardens he had traversed day by day
For six long years, led by a strong desire
To show his Brahman teachers his new light.
But ah! the change a little time had wrought!
A new-made stupa held their gathered dust,
While they had gone where all see eye to eye,
The darkness vanished and the river crossed.

Then turning sadly from this hallowed spot—
Hallowed by strivings for a higher life
More than by dust this little mound contained—
He sought beneath the spreading banyan-tree
His five companions, whom he lately left
Sad at his own departure from the way
The sacred Vedas and the fathers taught.
They too had gone, to Varanassi* gone,
High seat and centre of all sacred lore.

* Varanassi is an old name of Benares.

The day was well-nigh spent; his cave was near,
Where he had spent so many weary years,
And as he thither turned and upward climbed,
The shepherd's little child who watched the flock
His love had rescued from the bloody knife,
Upon a rock that rose above his path
Saw him pass by, and ran with eagerness
To bear the news. Joy filled that humble home.
They owed him all. The best they had they brought,
And offered it with loving gratitude.
The master ate, and as he ate he taught
These simple souls the great, the living truth
That love is more than costly sacrifice;
That daily duties done are highest praise;
That when life's duties end its sorrows end,
And higher joys await the pure in heart.
Their eager souls drank in his living words
As those who thirst drink in the living spring.
Then reverently they kissed his garment's hem,
And home returned, while he lay down to sleep.
And sweetly as a babe the master slept —
No doubts, no darkness, and no troubled dreams.
When rosy dawn next lit the eastern sky,
And morning's grateful coolness filled the air,
The master rose and his ablutions made.
With bowl and staff in hand he took his way
Toward Varanassi, hoping there to find
The five toward whom his earnest spirit yearned.

 Ten days have passed, and now the rising sun
That hangs above the distant mountain-peaks

Is mirrored back by countless rippling waves
That dance upon the Ganges' yellow stream,
Swollen by rains and melted mountain-snows,
And glorifies the thousand sacred fanes*
With gilded pinnacles and spires and domes
That rise in beauty on its farther bank,
While busy multitudes glide up and down
With lightly dipping oars and swelling sails.
And pilgrims countless as those shining waves,
From far and near, from mountain, hill and plain,
With dust and travel-stained, foot-sore, heart-sick,
Here came to bathe within the sacred stream,
Here came to die upon its sacred banks,
Seeking to wash the stains of guilt away,
Seeking to lay their galling burdens down.
Scoff not at these poor heavy-laden souls!
Blindly they seek, but that all-seeing Eye
That sees the tiny sparrow when it falls,
Is watching them, His angels hover near.
Who knows what visions meet their dying gaze?
Who knows what joys await those troubled hearts?

The ancient writings say that having naught
To pay the ferryman, the churl refused
To ferry him across the swollen stream,
When he was raised and wafted through the air.

---

* It can be no exaggeration to put the number of sacred edifices that burst upon Buddha's view as he first saw the holy city, at 1,000, as Phillips Brooks puts the present number of such edifices in Benares at 5,000.

What matter whether that all-powerful Love
Which moves the worlds, and bears with all our sins,
Sent him a chariot and steeds of fire,
Or moved the heart of some poor fisherman
To bear him over for a brother's sake?
All power is His, and men can never thwart
His all-embracing purposes of love.

Now past the stream and near the sacred grove
The deer-park called, the five saw him approach.
But grieved at his departure from the way
The ancient sages taught, said with themselves
They would not rise or do him reverence.
But as he nearer came, the tender love,
The holy calm that shone upon his face,
Made them at once forget their firm resolve.
They rose together, doing reverence,
And bringing water washed his way-soiled feet,
Gave him a mat, and said as with one voice:
"Master Gautama, welcome to our grove.
Here rest your weary limbs and share our shade.
Have you escaped from karma's fatal chains
And gained clear vision—found the living light?"

"Call me not master. Profitless to you
Six years have passed," the Buddha answered them,
"In doubt and darkness groping blindly on.
But now at last the day has surely dawned.
These eyes have seen Nirvana's sacred Sun,
And found the noble eightfold path that mounts

From life's low levels, mounts from death's dark
    shades
To changeless day, to never-ending rest."
Then with the prophet's newly kindled zeal,
Zeal for the truth his opened eyes had seen,
Zeal for the friends whose struggles he had shared,
Softened by sympathy and tender love,
He taught how selfishness was primal cause
Of every ill to which frail flesh is heir,
The poisoned fountain whence all sorrows flow,
The loathsome worm that coils about the root
And kills the germ of every springing joy,
The subtle foe that sows by night the tares
That quickly springing choke the goodly seed
Which left to grow would fill the daily life
With balmy fragrance and with precious fruit.
He showed that selfishness was life's sole bane
And love its great and sovereign antidote.
He showed how selfishness would change the child
From laughing innocence to greedy youth
And heartless manhood, cold and cruel age,
Which past the vale and stript of all disguise
Shrinks from the good, and eager slinks away
And seeks those dismal regions of the lost
His opened eyes with sinking heart had seen.
Then showed how love its guardian angel paints
Upon the cooing infant's smiling face,
Grows into gentle youth, and manhood rich
In works of helpfulness and brotherhood,
And ripens into mellow, sweet old age,
Childhood returned with all its gentleness,

Whose funeral-pile but lights the upward way
To those sweet fields his opened eyes had seen,
Those ever-widening mansions of delight.

Enwrapt the teacher taught the living truth;
Enwrapt the hearers heard his living words;
The night unheeded winged its rapid flight,
The morning found their souls from darkness free.

Six yellow robes Benares daily saw,
Six wooden alms-bowls held for daily food,
Six meeting sneers with smiles and hate with love,
Six watchers by the pilgrim's dying bed,
Six noble souls united in the work
Of giving light and hope and help to all.

A rich and noble youth, an only son,
Had seen Gautama passing through the streets,
A holy calm upon his noble face,
Had heard him tell the pilgrims by the stream,
Gasping for breath and breathing out their lives,
Of higher life and joys that never end;
And wearied, sated by the daily round
Of pleasure, luxury and empty show
That waste his days but fail to satisfy,
Yet fearing his companions' gibes and sneers,
He sought the master in the sacred grove
When the full moon was mirrored in the stream,
The sleeping city silvered by its light;
And there he lingered, drinking in his words,
Till night was passed and day was well-nigh spent.

The father, anxious for his absent son,
Had sought him through the night from street to
    street
In every haunt that youthful folly seeks,
And now despairing sought the sacred grove —
Perhaps by chance, perhaps led by the light
That guides the pigeon to her distant home —
And found him there. He too the Buddha heard,
And finding light, and filled with joy, he said:
"Illustrious master, you have found the way.
You place the upturned chalice on its base.
You fill with light the sayings dark of old.
You open blinded eyes to see the truth."

At length they thought of those poor hearts at
    home,
Mother and sister, watching through the night—
Waiting and watching through the livelong day,
Startled at every step, at every sound,
Startled at every bier that came in view
In that great city of the stranger dead,
That city where the living come to die —
And home returned when evening's rose and gold
Had faded from the sky, and myriad lamps
Danced on the sacred stream, and moon and stars
Hung quivering in its dark and silent depths.
But day by day returned, eager to hear
More of that truth that sweetens daily life,
Yet reaches upward to eternal day.

A marriage-feast,* three festivals in one,
Stirs to its depths Benares' social life.
A gorgeous sunset ushers in the night,
Sunset and city mirrored in the stream.
Broad marble steps upon the river-bank
Lead to a garden where a blaze of bloom,
A hedge of rose-trees, forms the outer wall;
An aged banyan-tree,† whose hundred trunks
Sustain a vaulted roof of living green
Which scarce a ray of noonday's sun can pierce,
The garden's vestibule and outer court;
While trees of every varied leaf and bloom
Shade many winding walks, where fountains fall
With liquid cadence into shining pools.
Above, beyond, the stately palace stands,
Inviting in, calling to peace and rest,
As if a soul dwelt in its marble form.

The darkness thickens, when a flood of light
Fills every recess, lighting every nook;
The garden hedge a wall of mellow light,
A line of lamps along the river's bank,
With lamps in every tree and lining every walk,
While lamps thick set surround each shining pool,
Weaving with rainbow tints the falling spray.

---

* In this marriage-feast three well-known incidents in the life of Buddha and his teachings on the three occasions are united.

† For the best description of the banyan-tree, see Lady Dufferin's account of the old tree at their out-of-town place in "Our Viceroyal Life in India," and "Two Years in Ceylon," by C. F. Gordon Cumming.

And now the palace through the darkness shines.
A thing of beauty traced with lines of light.*

   The guests arrive in light and graceful boats,
In gay gondolas such as Venice used,
With richest carpets, richest canopies,
And over walks with rose-leaves carpeted
Pass to the palace, whose wide open gates
Display within Benares' rank and wealth.
Proud Brahman lords and stately Brahman dames
And Brahman youth and beauty, all were there,
Of Aryan blood but bronzed by India's sun,
Not dressed like us, as very fashion-plates,
But clothed in flowing robes of softest wool
And finest silk, a harmony of shades,
Sparkling with gems, ablaze with precious stones.†
Three noble couples greet their gathering guests:
An aged Brahman and his aged wife,
For fifty years united in the bonds
Of wedded love, no harsh, unloving word
For all those happy years, their only fear
That death would break the bonds that bound their
    souls;
And next their eldest born, who sought his son,
And drank deep wisdom from the Buddha's lips,

---

   * Those who saw the illuminations at Chicago during the World's Fair, with lines of incandescent electric lights, can get a good idea of the great illuminations in India with innumerable oil lamps, and those who did not should read Lady Dufferin's charming description of them in "Our Viceroyal Life in India."

   † Lady Dufferin says that the viceroy never wearied in his admiration of the graceful flowing robes of the East as contrasted with our stiff, fashion-plate male attire.

And by his side that mother we have seen
Outwatch the night, whose sweet and earnest face
By five and twenty years of wedded love,
By five and twenty years of busy cares —
The cares of home, with all its daily joys —
Had gained that look of holy motherhood*
That millions worship on their bended knees
As highest emblem of eternal love ;
And last that sister whose untiring love
Watched by her mother through the weary hours,
Her fair young face all trust and happiness,
Before her, rainbow-tinted hopes and joys,
Life's dark and cold and cruel side concealed,
And by her side a noble Brahman youth,
Who saw in her his every hope fulfilled.

But where is now that erring, wandering son,
The pride of all these loyal, loving hearts,
Heir to this wealth and hope of this proud house ?

Seven clothed in coarsest yellow robes draw near
With heads close shorn and bare, unsandaled feet,
Alms-bowl on shoulder slung and staff in hand,
But moving with that gentle stateliness
That birth and blood, not wealth and effort, give,
All in the strength of manhood's early prime,
All heirs to wealth rejected, cast aside,
But all united in the holy cause

---

* "The good Lord could not be everywhere and therefore made mothers."—Jewish saying from the Talmud.

Of giving light and hope and help to all,
While earnest greetings from the evening's hosts
Show they are welcome and expected guests.

    Startled, the stately Brahmans turn aside.
"The heir has lost his reason," whispered they,
"And joined that wandering prince who late appeared
Among the yogis in the sacred grove,
Who thinks he sees the truth by inner sight,
Who fain would teach the wise, and claims to know
More than the fathers and the Vedas teach."
But as he nearer came, his stately form,
His noble presence and his earnest face,
Beaming with gentleness and holy love,
Hushed into silence every rising sneer.

    One of their number, wise in sacred lore,
Profoundly learned, in all the Vedas versed,
With courtly grace saluting Buddha, said :
"Our Brahman masters teach that many ways
Lead up to Brahma Loca, Brahma's rest,
As many roads from many distant lands
All meet before Benares' sacred shrines.
They say that he who learns the Vedas' hymns,
Performs the rites and prays the many prayers
That all the sages of the past have taught,
In Brahma's self shall be absorbed at last —
As all the streams from mountain, hill and plain,
That swell proud Gunga's broad and sacred stream,

At last shall mingle with the ocean's waves.
They say that Brahmans are a holy caste,
Of whiter skin and higher, purer blood,
From Brahma sprung, and Brahma's only heirs,
While you proclaim, if rumor speaks the truth,
That only one hard road to Brahma leads,
That every caste is pure, of common blood,
That all are brothers, all from Brahma sprung."

But Buddha, full of gentleness, replied:
"Ye call on Dyaus Pittar, Brahma, God,*
One God and Father, called by many names,
One God and Father, seen in many forms,
Seen in the tempest, mingling sea and sky,
The blinding sand-storm, changing day to night,
In gentle showers refreshing thirsty fields,
Seen in the sun whose rising wakes the world,
Whose setting calls a weary world to rest,
Seen in the deep o'erarching azure vault,
By day a sea of light, shining by night
With countless suns of countless worlds unseen,
Making us seem so little, God so great.
Ye say that Brahma dwells in purest light;
Ye say that Brahma's self is perfect love;
Ye pray to Brahma under many names

---

* Max Mueller calls attention to the remarkable fact that Dyaus Pittar, the highest name of deity among the ancient Hindoos, is the exact equivalent of Zeus Pater among the Greeks, Jupiter among the Romans, and of "Our Father who art in the heavens" in the divinely taught and holiest prayer of our own religion.

To give you Brahma Loca's perfect rest.*
Your prayers are vain unless your hearts are clean.
For how can darkness dwell with perfect light?
And how can hatred dwell with perfect love?
The slandering tongue, that stirs up strife and hate,
The grasping hand, that takes but never gives,
The lying lips, the cold and cruel heart,
Whence bitterness and wars and murders spring,
Can ne'er by prayers to Brahma Loca climb.†
The pure in heart alone with Brahma dwell.
Ye say that Brahmans are a holy caste,
From Brahma sprung and Brahma's only heirs;
But yet in Bactria, whence our fathers came,
And where their brothers and our kindred dwell,
No Brahman ever wore the sacred cord.
Has mighty Brahma there no son, no heir?
The Brahman mother suffers all the pangs
Kshatriyas, Sudras or the Vassas feel.
The Brahman's body, when the soul has fled,

---

*How any one can think that Buddha did not believe in a Supreme Being in the face and light of the wonderful Sutra or sermon of which the text is but a condensation or abstract, is to me unaccountable. It is equally strange that any one should suppose he regarded Nirvana, which is but another name for Brahma Loca, as meaning annihilation.

To be sure he used the method afterwards adopted by Socrates, and now known as the Socratic method, of appealing to the unquestioned belief of the Brahmans themselves as the foundation of his argument in support of that fundamental truth of all religions, that the pure in heart alone can see God. But to suppose that he was using arguments to convince them that he did not believe himself, is a libel on one whose absolute truthfulness and sincerity admit of no question.

† "He prayeth best who loveth best
Both man and bird and beast."
—Rime of the Ancient Mariner.

A putrid mass, defiles the earth and air,
Vile as the Sudras or the lowest beasts.
The Brahman murderer, libertine or thief
Ye say will be reborn in lowest beast,
While some poor Sudra, full of gentleness
And pity, charity and trust and love,
May rise to Brahma Loca's perfect rest.
Why boast of caste, that seems so little worth
To raise the soul or ward off human ill?
Why pray for what we do not strive to gain?
Like merchants on the swollen Ganges' bank
Praying the farther shore to come to them,
Taking no steps, seeking no means, to cross.
Far better strive to cast out greed and hate.
Live not for self, but live for others' good.
Indulge no bitter speech, no bitter thoughts.
Help those in need; give freely what we have.
Kill not, steal not, and ever speak the truth.
Indulge no lust; taste not the maddening bowl
That deadens sense and stirs all base desires;
And live in charity and gentle peace,
Bearing all meekly, loving those who hate.
This is the way to Brahma Loca's rest.
And ye who may, come, follow after me.
Leave wealth and home and all the joys of life,
That we may aid a sad and suffering world
In sin and sorrow groping blindly on,
Becoming poor that others may be rich,
Wanderers ourselves to lead the wanderers home.
And ye who stay, ever remember this:

That hearth is Brahma's altar where love reigns,
That house is Brahma's temple where love dwells.
Ye ask, my aged friends, if death can break
The bonds that bind your souls in wedded love.
Fear not; death has no power to conquer love.
Go hand in hand till death shall claim his own,
Then hand in hand ascend Nirvana's heights,
There, hand in hand, heart beating close to heart,
Enter that life whose joys shall never end,
Perennial youth succeeding palsied age,
Mansions of bliss for this poor house of clay,
Labors of love instead of toil and tears."

   He spoke, and many to each other said:
"Why hear this babbler rail at sacred things —
Our caste, our faith, our prayers and sacred
    hymns?"
And strode away in proud and sovereign scorn;
While some with gladness heard his solemn words,
All soon forgotten in the giddy whirl
Of daily business, daily joys and cares.
But some drank in his words with eager ears,
And asked him many questions, lingering long,
And often sought him in the sacred grove
To hear his burning words of living truth.
And day by day some noble Brahman youth
Forsook his wealth, forsook his home and friends,
And took the yellow robe and begging-bowl
To ask for alms where all had given him place,
Meeting with gentleness the rabble's gibes,

Meeting with smiles the Brahman's haughty scorn.
Thus, day by day, this school of prophets grew.
Beneath the banyan's columned, vaulted shade,
All earnest learners at the master's feet,
Until the city's busy, bustling throng
Had come to recognize the yellow robe,
The poor to know its wearer as a friend,
The sick and suffering as a comforter,
While to the dying pilgrim's glazing eyes
He seemed a messenger from higher worlds
Come down to raise his sinking spirit up
And guide his trembling steps to realms of rest.

A year has passed, and of this growing band
Sixty are rooted, grounded in the faith,
Willing to do whate'er the master bids,
Ready to go where'er the master sends,
Eager to join returning pilgrim-bands
And bear the truth to India's farthest bounds.

With joy the master saw their burning zeal,
So free from selfishness, so full of love,
And thought of all those blindly groping souls
To whom these messengers would bear the light.

"Go," said the master, "each a different way.
Go teach the common brotherhood of man.
Preach Dharma, preach the law of perfect love,
One law for high and low, for rich and poor.
Teach all to shun the cudgel and the sword,

And treat with kindness every living thing.
Teach them to shun all theft and craft and greed,
All bitter thoughts, and false and slanderous speech
That severs friends and stirs up strife and hate.
Revere your own, revile no brother's faith.
The light you see is from Nirvana's Sun,
Whose rising splendors promise perfect day.
The feeble rays that light your brother's path
Are from the selfsame Sun, by falsehoods hid,
The lingering shadows of the passing night.
Chide none with ignorance, but teach the truth
Gently, as mothers guide their infants' steps,
Lest your rude manners drive them from the way
That leads to purity and peace and rest —
As some rude swain in some sequestered vale,
Who thinks the visual line that girts him round
The world's extreme, would meet with sturdy blows
One rudely charging him with ignorance,
Yet gently led to some commanding height,
Whence he could see the Himalayan peaks,
The rolling hills and India's spreading plains,
With joyful wonder views the glorious scene.
Pause not to break the idols of the past.
Be guides and leaders, not iconoclasts.
Their broken idols shock their worshipers,
But led to light they soon forgotten lie."

    One of their number, young and strong and brave,
A merchant ere he took the yellow robe,
Had crossed the frozen Himalayan heights

And found a race, alien in tongue and blood,
Gentle as children in their daily lives,
Untaught as children in all sacred things,
Living in wagons, wandering o'er the steppes,
To-day all shepherds, tending countless flocks,
To-morrow warriors, cruel as the grave,
Building huge monuments of human heads —
Fearless, resistless, with the cyclone's speed
Leaving destruction in their bloody track,
Who drove the Aryan from his native plains
To seek a home in Europe's trackless wastes.
He yearned to seek these children of the wilds,
And teach them peace and gentleness and love.*
"But, Purna," said the master, "they are fierce.
How will you meet their cruelty and wrath?"
Purna replied, "With gentleness and love."
"But," said the master, "they may beat and wound."
"And I will give them thanks to spare my life."
"But with slow tortures they may even kill."
"I with my latest breath will bless their names,
So soon to free me from this prison-house
And send me joyful to the other shore."
"Then," said the master, "Purna, it is well.

---

*Whether the Tartars were "the savage tribes" to whom Purna, one of the sixty, was sent, may admit of question, but it is certain that long before the Christian era the whole country north of the Himalayas was thoroughly Buddhist, and the unwearied missionaries of that great faith had penetrated so far west that they met Alexander's army and boldly told him that war was wrong; and they had penetrated east to the confines of China.

Armed with such patience, seek these savage tribes.
Thyself delivered, free from karma's chains
These souls enslaved; thyself consoled, console
These restless children of the desert wastes;
Thyself this peaceful haven having reached,
Guide these poor wanderers to the other shore."

With many counsels, many words of cheer,
He on their mission sent his brethren forth,
Armed with a prophet's zeal, a brother's love,
A martyr's courage, and the Christian's hope
That when life's duties end, its trials end,
And higher life awaits those faithful found.

The days pass on; and now the rising sun
Looks down on bands of pilgrims homeward bound,
Some moving north, some south, some east, some west,
Toward every part of India's vast expanse,
One clothed in orange robes with every band
To guide their kindred on the upward road.

But Purna joined the merchants he had led,
Not moved by thirst for gain, but love for man,
To seek the Tartar on his native steppes.

Meanwhile the master with diminished band
Crossing the Ganges, backward wends his way
Toward Rajagriha, and the vulture-peak
Where he had spent so many weary years,

Whither he bade the brothers gather in*
When summer's rains should bring the time for rest.

*The large gatherings of the Buddhist brotherhoods everywhere spoken of in the writings can only be accounted for on the supposition, which is more than a supposition, that they came to him in the rainy season, when they could do but little in their missions; and the substantial unity of the Buddhist faith can only be accounted for on the supposition that his instructions were constantly renewed at these gatherings and their errors corrected.

BOOK VIII.

Northward the noble Purna took his way
Till India's fields and plains were lost to view,
Then through the rugged foot-hills upward climbed,
And up a gorge by rocky ramparts walled,
Through which a mighty torrent thundered down,
Their treacherous way along the torrent's brink,
Or up the giddy cliffs where one false step
Would plunge them headlong in the raging stream,
Passing from cliff to cliff, their bridge of ropes
Swung high above the dashing, roaring waves.
At length they cross the frozen mountain-pass,
O'er wastes of snow by furious tempests swept,
And cross a desert where no bird or beast
Is ever seen, and where their way is marked
By bleaching bones strewn thick along their track.*

Some perished by the way, and some turned back,
While some of his companions persevered,

---

* I have substantially followed the description of this fearful route given by Fa Hian, the Chinese Buddhist pilgrim, who passed by it from China to India.

Cheered on by Purna's never-flagging zeal,
And by the master's words from Purna's lips,
Until they reached the outmost wandering tribes
Of that great race that he had come to save.
With joy received, these wandering tribes their guides —
For love makes friends where selfishness breeds strife —
They soon are led to where their kindred dwell.
They saw the vanity of chasing wealth
Through hunger, danger, desolation, death.
They felt a power sustaining Purna's steps —
A power unseen yet ever hovering near —
They saw the truth of Buddha's burning words
That selfishness and greed drag down the soul,
While love can nerve the feeblest arm with strength,
And asked that Purna take them as his aids.

But ere brave Purna reached his journey's end,
Near many hamlets, many Indian towns,
The moon, high risen to mark the noon of night,
Through many sacred fig-tree's rustling leaves*
Sent trembling rays with trembling shadows mixed
Upon a noble youth in orange robes,
His alms-bowl by his side, stretched out in sleep,
Dreaming, perchance, of some Benares maid,
Perchance of home and joys so lately left.

* Like the aspen, the leaf of the sacred fig-tree is always trembling.—"Two Years in Ceylon," Cumming.

Meanwhile the master with his little band
Toward Rajagriha backward wends his way,
Some village tree their nightly resting-place,
Until they reached the grove that skirts the base
Of that bold mountain called the vulture-peak,
Through which the lotus-covered Phalgu glides,
O'erarched with trees festooned with trailing vines,
While little streams leap down from rock to rock,
Cooling the verdant slopes and fragrant glades,
And vines and shrubs and trees of varied bloom
Loaded the air with odors rich and sweet,
And where that sacred fig-tree spread its shade
Above the mound that held the gathered dust
Of those sage Brahmans who had sought to aid
The young prince struggling for a clearer light,
And where that banyan-tree for ages grew,
So long the home of those five noble youths,
Now sundered far, some tree when night may fall
Their resting-place, their robe and bowl their all,
Their only food chance gathered day by day,
Preaching the common brotherhood of man,
Teaching the law of universal love,
Bearing the light to those in darkness sunk,
Lending a helping hand to those in need,
Teaching the strong that gentleness is great.
And through this grove where many noble souls
Were seeking higher life and clearer light,
He took his well-known way, and reached his cave
Just as the day was fading into night,
And myriad stars spangled the azure vault,

And myriad lamps that through the darkness
    shone
Revealed the city that the night had veiled,
Where soon their weary limbs were laid to rest ;
But through the silent hour preceding day,
Before the jungle-cock announced the dawn,
All roused from sleep in meditation sat.
But when the sun had set the east aglow,
And roused the birds to sing their matin-songs,
And roused the lowing herds to call their mates,
And roused a sleeping world to daily toil,
Their matins chanted, their ablutions made,
With bowl and staff in hand they took their way
Down to the city for their daily alms.

But earlier steps had brushed their dewy path.
From out the shepherd's cottage loving eyes
Had recognized the master's stately form,
And love-winged steps had borne the joyful news
That he, the poor man's advocate and friend,
The sweet-voiced messenger of peace and love,
The prince become a beggar for their sake,
So long expected, now at last returns.
From door to door the joyful tidings spread,
And old and young from every cottage came.
The merchant left his wares without a guard ;
The housewife left her pitcher at the well ;
The loom was idle and the anvil still ;
The money-changer told his coins alone,
While all the multitude went forth to meet
Their servant-master and their beggar-prince.

Some brought the garden's choicest treasures
   forth,
Some gathered lotuses from Phalgu's stream,
Some climbed the trees to pluck their varied bloom,
While children gathered every wayside flower
To strew his way — their lover, savior, guide.

   King Bimbasara from his watch-tower saw
The wild commotion and the moving throng,
And sent swift messengers to learn the cause.
With winged feet through vacant streets they flew,
And through the gates and out an avenue
Where aged trees that grew on either side,
Their giant branches interlocked above,
Made nature's gothic arch and densest shade,
While gentle breezes, soft as if they came
From devas' hovering wings, rustle the leaves
And strew the way with showers of falling bloom,
As if they, voiceless, felt the common joy.
And there they found the city's multitudes,
Not as in tumult, armed with clubs and staves,
And every weapon ready to their hands,
But stretching far on either side the way,
Their flower-filled hands in humble reverence
   joined,
The only sound a murmur, "There he comes!"
While every eye was turned in loving gaze
Upon a little band in yellow robes
Who now drew near from out the sacred grove.
The master passed with calm, majestic grace,
Stately and tall, one arm and shoulder bare,

With head close shorn and bare unsandaled feet ;
His noble brow, the wonder of his age,
Not clothed in terror like Olympic Jove's —
For love, not anger, beamed from out those eyes,
Changing from clearest blue to softest black,
That seem to show unfathomed depths within,
With tears of holy pity glittering now
For those poor souls come forth to honor him,
All sheep without a shepherd groping on.
The messengers with reverence let him pass,
Then hastened back to tell the waiting king
That he who dwelt so long upon the hill,
The prince who stopped the bloody sacrifice,
With other holy rishis had returned,
Whom all received with reverence and joy.
The king with keenest pleasure heard their words.
That noble form, that calm, majestic face,
Had never faded from his memory.
His words of wisdom, words of tender love,
Had often stayed his hands when raised to strike,
Had often put a bridle on his tongue
When harsh and bitter words leaped to his lips,
And checked those cruel acts of sudden wrath
That stain the annals of the greatest kings,
Until the people to each other said :
" How mild and gentle our good king has grown !"
And when he heard this prince had now returned,
In flower-embroidered purple robes arrayed,
With all the pomp and circumstance of state,
Followed by those who ever wait on power,
He issued forth and climbed the rugged hill

Until he reached the cave where Buddha sat,
Calm and majestic as the rounded moon
That moves serene along its heavenly path.
Greeting each other with such royal grace
As fits a prince greeting a brother prince,
The king inquired why he had left his home?
Why he, a Chakravartin's only son,
Had left his palace for a lonely cave,
Wore coarsest cloth instead of royal robes,
And for a scepter bore a begging-bowl?
"Youth." said the king, "with full and bounding pulse,
Youth is the time for boon companionship,
The time for pleasure, when all pleasures please;
Manhood, the time for gaining wealth and power;
But as the years creep on, the step infirm,
The arm grown feeble and the hair turned gray,
'Tis time to mortify the five desires,
To give religion what of life is left,
And look to heaven when earth begins to pall.
I would not use my power to hold you here,
But offer half my kingdom for your aid
To govern well and use my power aright."
The prince with gentle earnestness replied:
"O king, illustrious and world-renowned!
Your noble offer through all coming time
Shall be remembered. Men will praise an act
By likening it to Bimbasara's gift.
You offer me the half of your domain.
I in return beseech you share with me
Better than wealth, better than kingly power,

The peace and joy that follows lusts subdued.
Wait not on age — for age brings feebleness —
But this great battle needs our utmost strength.
If you will come, then welcome to our cave;
If not, may wisdom all your actions guide.
Ruling your empire in all righteousness,
Preserve your country and protect her sons.
Sadly I leave you, great and gracious king,
But my work calls — a world that waits for light.
In yonder sacred grove three brothers dwell—
Kasyapa, Gada, Nadi, they are called;
Three chosen vessels for the perfect law,
Three chosen lamps to light a groping world,
Who worship now the gross material fire
Which burns and wastes but fails to purify.
I go to tell them of Nirvana's Sun,
Perennial source of that undying flame,
The fire of love, consuming lust and hate
As forest fires devour the crackling thorns,
Until the soul is purified from sin,
And sorrow, birth and death are left behind."

He found Kasyapa as the setting sun
Was sinking low behind the western hills,
And somber shadows darkened Phalgu's vale,
And asked a place to pass the gathering night.
"Here is a grotto, cooled by trickling streams
And overhanging shades, fit place for sleep,"
Kasyapa said, "that I would gladly give;
But some fierce Naga nightly haunts the spot

Whose poisoned breath no man can breathe and
    live."
"Fear not for me," the Buddha answered him,
"For I this night will make my dwelling there."
"Do as you will," Kasyapa doubtful said,
"But much I fear some dire catastrophe."
Now mighty Mara, spirit of the air,
The prince of darkness, roaming through the earth
Had found this grotto in the sacred grove,
And as a Naga there kept nightly watch
For those who sought deliverance from his power,
Who, when the master calmly took his seat,
Belched forth a flood of poison, foul and black,
And with hot, burning vapors filled the cave.
But Buddha sat unmoved, serene and calm
As Brahma sits amid the kalpa fires
That burn the worlds but cannot harm his heaven.
While Mara, knowing Buddha, fled amazed
And left the Naga coiled in Buddha's bowl.*
Kasyapa, terrified, beheld the flames,
And when the first faint rays of dawn appeared
With all his fearful followers sought the cave,
And found the master not consumed to dust,
But full of peace, aglow with perfect love.
Kasyapa, full of wonder, joyful said:
"I, though a master, have no power like this
To conquer groveling lusts and evil beasts."
Then Buddha taught the source of real power,

---

* This is Asvaghosha's version, but the Sanchi inscriptions make the Naga or cobra rise up behind Buddha and extend its hood over his head as a shelter.

The power of love to fortify the soul,
Until Kasyapa gathered all his stores,
His sacred vessels, sacrificial robes,
And cast them in the Phalgu passing near.
His brothers saw them floating down the stream,
And winged with fear made haste to learn the
    cause.
They too the master saw, and heard his words,
And all convinced received the perfect law,
And with their followers joined the Buddha's band.

    The days pass on, and in the bamboo-grove
A great vihara as by magic rose,
Built by the king for Buddha's growing band,
A spacious hall where all might hear his words,
And little cells where each might take his rest,
A school and rest-house through the summer rains.

    But soon the monsoons from the distant seas
Bring gathering clouds to veil the brazen sky,
While nimble lightnings dart their blinding flames,
And rolling thunders shake the trembling hills,
And heaven's downpourings drench the thirsty
    earth —
The master's seed-time when the people rest.
For now the sixty from their distant fields
Have gathered in to trim their lamps afresh
And learn new wisdom from the master's lips —
All but brave Purna on the Tartar steppes
Where summer is the fittest time for toil,
When India's rains force India's sons to rest.

The new vihara and the bamboo-grove
King Bimbasara to the master gave,
Where day by day he taught his growing school,
While rills, grown torrents, leap from rock to rock,
And Phalgu's swollen stream sweeps down the vale.

That Saraputra after called the Great
Had seen these new-come youths in yellow robes
Passing from street to street to ask for alms,
Receiving coarsest food with gentle thanks —
Had seen them meet the poor and sick and old
With kindly words and ever-helpful hands —
Had seen them passing to the bamboo-grove
Joyful as bridegrooms soon to meet their brides.
He, Vashpa and Asvajit met one day,
Whom he had known beneath the banyan-tree,
Two of the five who first received the law,
Now clothed in yellow, bearing begging-bowls,
And asked their doctrine, who their master was,
That they seemed joyful, while within the grove
All seemed so solemn, self-absorbed and sad.
They bade him come and hear the master's words,
And when their bowls were filled, he followed them,
And heard the living truth from Buddha's lips,
And said : "The sun of wisdom has arisen.
What further need of our poor flickering lamps?"
And with Mugallan joined the master's band.

And now five strangers from the Tartar steppes,
Strangers in form and features, language, dress,
Guided by one as strange in dress as they,

Weary and foot-sore, passed within the gates
Of Rajagriha, while the rising sun
Was still concealed behind the vulture-peak,
A laughing-stock to all the idle crowd,
Whom noisy children followed through the streets
As thoughtless children follow what is strange,
Until they met the master asking alms,
Who with raised hand and gentle, mild rebuke
Hushed into silence all their noisy mirth.
"These are our brothers," Buddha mildly said.
"Weary and worn they come from distant lands,
And ask for kindness — not for mirth and jeers."
They knew at once that calm, majestic face,
That voice as sweet as Brahma's, and those eyes
Beaming with tender, all-embracing love,
Of which, while seated round their argol fires
In their black tents, brave Purna loved to tell,
And bowed in worship at the master's feet.
He bade them rise, and learned from whence they came,
And led them joyful to the bamboo-grove,
Where some brought water from the nearest stream
To bathe their festered feet and weary limbs,
While some brought food and others yellow robes —
Fitter for India's heat than skins and furs —
All welcoming their new-found friends who came
From distant lands, o'er desert wastes and snows,
To see the master, hear the perfect law,
And bring the message noble Purna sent.

The months pass on ; the monsoons cease to blow,
The thunders cease to roll, the rains to pour ;
The earth, refreshed, is clothed with living green,
And flowers burst forth where all was parched and
   bare,
And busy toil succeeds long days of rest.
The time for mission work has come.
The brethren, now to many hundreds grown,
Where'er the master thought it best were sent.
The strongest and the bravest volunteered
To answer Purna's earnest call for help,
And clothed in fitting robes for piercing cold
They scale the mountains, pass the desert wastes,
Their guide familiar with their terrors grown ;
While some return to their expectant flocks,
And some are sent to kindred lately left,
And some to strangers dwelling near or far —
All bearing messages of peace and love —
Until but few in yellow robes remain,
And single footfalls echo through that hall
Where large assemblies heard the master's words.
A few are left, not yet confirmed in faith ;
And those five brothers from the distant north
Remain to learn the sacred tongue and lore,
While Saraputra and Kasyapa stay
To aid the master in his special work.

From far Kosala, rich Sudata came,
Friend of the destitute and orphans called.
In houses rich, and rich in lands and gold,
But richer far in kind and gracious acts,

Who stopped in Rajagriha with a friend.
But when he learned a Buddha dwelt so near,
And heard the gracious doctrine he proclaimed,
That very night he sought the bamboo-grove,
While roofs and towers were silvered by the moon,
And silent streets in deepest shadows lay,
And bamboo-plumes seemed waving silver sprays,
And on the ground the trembling shadows played.
Humble in mind but great in gracious deeds,
Of earnest purpose but of simple heart,
The master saw in him a vessel fit
For righteousness, and bade him stay and learn
His rules of grace that bring Nirvana's rest.
And first of all the gracious master said:
"This restless nature and this selfish world
Is all a phantasy and empty show;
Its life is lust, its end is pain and death.
Waste not your time in speculations deep
Of whence and why. One thing we surely know:
Each living thing must have a living cause,
And mind from mind and not from matter springs;
While love, which like an endless golden chain
Binds all in one, is love in every link,
Up from the sparrow's nest, the mother's heart,
Through all the heavens to Brahma's boundless
  love.
And lusts resisted, daily duties done,
Unite our lives to that unbroken chain
Which draws us up to heaven's eternal rest."
And through the night they earnestly communed,
Until Sudata saw the living truth

In rising splendor, like the morning sun,
And doubts and errors all are swept away
As gathering clouds are swept by autumn's winds.

   Bowing in reverence, Sudata said:
"I know the Buddha never seeks repose,
But gladly toils to give to others rest.
O that my people, now in darkness sunk,
Might see the light and hear the master's words!
I dwell in King Pasenit's distant realm —
A king renowned, a country fair and rich —
And yearn to build a great vihara there."
The master, knowing well Sudata's heart
And his unselfish charity, replied:
"Some give in hope of greater gifts returned;
Some give to gain a name for charity;
Some give to gain the rest and joy of heaven,
Some to escape the woes and pains of hell.
Such giving is but selfishness and greed,
But he who gives without a selfish thought
Has entered on the noble eightfold path,
Is purified from anger, envy, hate.
The bonds of pain and sorrow are unloosed;
The way to rest and final rescue found.
Let your hands do what your kind heart desires."

   Hearing this answer, he departs with joy,
And Buddha with him Saraputra sent.
Arriving home, he sought a pleasant spot,
And found the garden of Pasenit's son,
And sought the prince, seeking to buy the ground.

But he refused to sell, yet said in jest :
"Cover the grove with gold, the ground is yours."
Forthwith Sudata spread his yellow coin.
But Gata said, caught by his thoughtless jest :
"Spread not your gold—I will not sell the ground."
"Not sell the ground ?" Sudata sharply said,
"Why then said you, 'Fill it with yellow gold'?"
And both contending sought a magistrate.
But Gata, knowing well his earnestness,
Asked why he sought the ground ; and when he learned,
He said : "Keep half your gold ; the land is yours,
But mine the trees, and jointly we will build
A great vihara for the Buddha's use."
The work begun was pressed both night and day ;
Lofty it rose, in just proportions built,
Fit for the palace of a mighty king.
The people saw this great vihara rise,
A stately palace for a foreign prince,
And said in wonder : "What strange thing is this ?
Our king to welcome thus a foreign king
To new-made palaces, and not with war
And bloody spears and hands to new-made graves,
As was his father's wont in times gone by ?"
Yet all went forth to meet this coming prince,
And see a foreign monarch's royal pomp,
But heard no trumpeting of elephants,
Nor martial music, nor the neigh of steeds,
But saw instead a little band draw near
In yellow robes, with dust and travel-stained ;
But love, that like a holy halo crowned

That dusty leader's calm, majestic brow,
Hushed into silence every rising sneer.
And when Sudata met this weary band,
And to the prince's garden led their way,
They followed on, their hands in reverence joined,
To where the stately new vihara rose,
Enbowered in giant trees of every kind
That India's climate grows, while winding streams
Along their flowery banks now quiet flow,
Now leap from rocks, now spread in shining pools
With lotuses and lilies overspread,
While playing fountains with their falling spray
Spread grateful coolness, and a blaze of bloom
From myriad opening flowers perfumes the air,
And myriad birds that sought this peaceful spot
Burst forth in every sweet and varied song
That India's fields and groves and gardens know.
And there Sudata bowed on bended knee,
And from a golden pitcher water poured,
The sign and sealing of their gift of love
Of this vihara, Gatavana called,
A school and rest-house for the Buddha's use,
And for the brotherhood throughout the world.
Buddha received it with the fervent prayer
That it might give the kingdom lasting peace.

   Unlike Sudata's self, Sudata's king
Believed religion but a comely cloak
To hide besetting sins from public view,
And sought the master in his new retreat
To talk religion and to act a part,

And greetings ended, said in solemn wise:
"Uneasy lies the head that wears a crown;
But my poor kingdom now is doubly blest
In one whose teachings purify the soul
And give the highest and the humblest rest,
As all are cleansed who bathe in Rapti's stream."
But Buddha saw through all this outer show
His real purposes and inner life:
The love of pleasure blighting high resolve,
The love of money, root of every ill,
That sends its poison fibers through the soul
And saps its life and wastes its vital strength.
"The Tathagata only shows the way
To purity and rest," the master said.
"There is a way to darkness out of light,
There is a way to light from deepest gloom.
They only gain the goal who keep the way.
Harsh words and evil deeds to sorrow lead
As sure as shadows on their substance wait.
For as we sow, so also shall we reap.
Boast not o'ermuch of kingly dignity.
A king most needs a kind and loving heart
To love his subjects as an only son,
To aid — not injure, comfort — not oppress,
Their help, protector, father, friend and guide.
Such kings shall live beloved and die renowned,
Whose works shall welcome them to heavenly rest."
The king, convicted, heard his solemn words
That like an arrow pierced his inmost life.
To him religion ceased to be a show
Of chants and incense, empty forms and creeds,

But stood a living presence in his way
To check his blind and headlong downward course,
And lead him to the noble eightfold path,
That day by day and step by step shall lead
To purity and peace and heavenly rest.

    Kapilavastu's king, Suddhodana,
His step grown feeble, snowy white his hair,
By cares oppressed and sick with hope deferred,
For eight long years had waited for his son.
But sweet Yasodhara, in widow's weeds,
Her love by sorrow only purified
As fire refines the gold by dross debased,
Though tender memories bring unbidden tears,
Wasted no time in morbid, selfish grief,
But sought in care for others her own cure.
Both son and daughter to the aged king,
She aids with counsels, soothes with tender care.
Father and mother to her little son,
She lavishes on him a double love.
And oft on mercy's missions going forth,
Shunning the pomp and show of royal state,
Leading Rahula, prattling by her side,
The people saw her pass with swelling hearts,
As if an angel clothed in human form.

    And now strange rumors reach the public ear,
By home-bound pilgrims from Benares brought
And merchantmen from Rajagriha come,
That there a holy rishi had appeared
Whom all believed a very living Buddh,

While kings and peoples followed after him.
These rumors reached the sweet Yasodhara,
And stirred these musings in her watchful heart:
"Stately and tall they say this rishi is,
Gentle to old and young, to rich and poor,
And filled with love for every living thing.
But who so gentle, stately, tall and grand
As my Siddartha? Who so full of love?
And he has found the light Siddartha sought!
It must be he — my own, my best beloved!
And surely he will hither come, and bring
To his poor people, now in darkness sunk,
That living light he left his home to seek."

As the same sun that makes the cedars grow
And sends their vital force through giant oaks,
Clothes fields with green and decks the wayside
    flower,
And crowns the autumn with its golden fruits,
So that same love which swept through Buddha's
    soul
And drove him from his home to seek and save,
Warmed into brighter glow each lesser love
Of home and people, father, wife and child,*
And often through those long and troubled years

---

*Some Buddhists teach that Buddha had conquered all human affections, and even enter into apologies for a show of affection for his wife, one of the most elaborate of which Arnold, in the "Light of Asia," puts into his own mouth; but this is no more like the teachings of Buddha than the doctrine of infant damnation is like the teachings of Him who said: "Suffer the little children to come unto me, and forbid them not; for of such is the kingdom of God."

He felt a burning longing to return.
And now, when summer rains had ceased to fall,
And his disciples were again sent forth,
Both love and duty with united voice
Bade him revisit his beloved home,
And Saraputra and Kasyapa joined
The master wending on his homeward way,
While light-winged rumor bore Yasodhara
This joyful news: "The holy rishi comes."

Without the southern gate a garden lay,
Lumbini called, by playing fountains cooled,
With shaded walks winding by banks of flowers,
Whose mingled odors load each passing breeze.
Thither Yasodhara was wont to go,
For there her lord and dearest love was born,
And there they passed full many happy days.
The southern road skirted this garden's wall,
While on the other side were suburb huts
Where toiling poor folk and the base-born dwell.
And near this wall a bright pavilion rose,
Whence she could see each passer by the way.
One morning, after days of patient watch,
She saw approach along this dusty road
Three seeming pilgrims, clothed in yellow robes,
Presenting at each humble door their bowls
For such poor food as these poor folk could give.
As they drew near, a growing multitude,
From every cottage swelled, followed their steps,
Gazing with awe upon the leader's face,
While each to his companion wondering said:

"Who ever saw a rishi such as this,
Who calls us brothers, whom the Brahmans scorn?"
But sweet Yasodhara, with love's quick sight,
Knew him she waited for, and forth she rushed,
Crying: "Siddartha, O my love! my lord!"
And prostrate in the dust she clasped his feet.
He gently raised and pressed her to his heart
In one most tender, loving, long embrace.
By that embrace her every heartache cured,
She calmly said: "Give me a humble part
In your great work, for though my hands are weak
My heart is strong, and my weak hands can bear
The cooling cup to fever's burning lips;
My mother's heart has more than room enough
For many outcasts, many helpless waifs."
And there in presence of that base-born throng,
Who gazed with tears and wonder on the scene,
And in a higher presence, who can doubt
He made her first of that great sisterhood,
Since through the ages known in every land,
Who gently raise the dying soldier's head,
Where cruel war is mangling human limbs;
Who smooth the pillow, bathe the burning brow
Of sick and helpless strangers taken in;
Whose tender care has made the orphans' home,
For those poor waifs who know no mother's love.
Then toward the palace they together went
To their Rahula and the aged king,
While streets were lined and doors and windows filled
With eager gazers at the prince returned

In coarsest robes, with closely shaven head,
Returned a Buddha who went forth a prince.

   Through all these troubled, weary, waiting years,
The king still hoped to see his son return
In royal state, with kings for waiting-men,
To rule a willing world as king of kings.
But now that son enters his palace-gates
In coarsest beggar-garb, his alms-bowl filled
With Sudras' leavings for his daily food.
The king with mingled grief and anger said :
"Is this the end of all our cherished hopes,
The answer to such lofty prophecies,
To see the heir of many mighty kings
Enter his kingdom like a beggar-tramp ?
This the return for all the patient love
Of sweet Yasodhara, and this the way
To teach his duty to your royal son ?"
The prince with reverence kissed his father's hand,
Bent loving eyes upon his troubled brow
That banished all his bitterness and said :
"How hard it is to give up cherished hopes
I know full well. I know a father's love.
Your love for me I for Rahula feel,
And who can better know that deepest love
Whose tendrils round my very heartstrings twine !
But crores of millions, with an equal love,
Fathers and mothers, children, husbands, wives,
In doubt and darkness groping blindly on,
Cry out for help. Not lack of love for you,
Or my Rahula or Yasodhara,

But love for them drove me to leave my home.
The greatest kingdoms are like ocean's foam,
A moment white upon the crested wave.
The longest life is but a passing dream,
Whose changing scenes but fill a moment's space.
But these poor souls shall live in joy or woe
While nations rise and fall and kalpas pass,
And this proud city crumbles to decay
Till antiquarians search its site in vain,
And beasts shall burrow where this palace stands.
Not for the pleasures of a passing day,
Like shadows flitting ere you point their place,
Not for the transient glories of a king,
Now clothed in scarlet but to-morrow dust,
Can I forget those loving, living souls,
Groping in darkness, vainly asking help."
And then he showed the noble eightfold path
From life's low levels to Nirvana's heights,
While king and people on the master gazed,
Whose face, beaming with pure, unselfish love,
Transfigured seemed; and many noble youth,
And chief Ananda, the Beloved called,
Forsook their gay companions and the round
Of youthful sports, and joined the master's band.
And as he spoke, crores more than mortals saw
Gathered to hear, and King Suddhodana
And sweet Yasodhara entered the path.

www.ingramcontent.com/pod-product-compliance
Lightning Source LLC
Chambersburg PA
CBHW032155160426
43197CB00008B/926